NOT RECOMMENDED FOR CHILDREN UNDER 3 YEARS OF AGE

Betty

BA**50p**G
SET

BAKE LIKE MOTHER
WITH THESE REALI-
STIC UTENSILS

FLOUR

DISHY

MADE IN HONG KONG

No. 411

Copyright ©2000 by Kevin Gould

First published in Great Britain in 2000
by Hodder and Stoughton
A division of Hodder Headline

10 9 8 7 6 5 4 3 2 1

A CIP catalogue record for this title is available from
the British Library.

ISBN 0 340 75095 2

Printed and bound in Great Britain
by The Bath Press

design@michaelnash.co.uk

Photography by
Annabel Elston (pages 15, 22, 23, 36, 42, 43, 56, 57,
62, 63, 79, 80, 81, 97, 104, 118, 119, 126, 136,
143, 154, 160, 167, 175, 181, 184, 192, 193, 194,
195, 196, 197, 199, 201); **Jason Lowe** (pages 16, 17,
19, 20, 24, 26, 33, 34, 38, 39, 44, 52, 55, 58, 61,
66, 72, 75, 76, 92, 93, 99, 100, 108, 116, 121, 122,
123, 124, 128, 129, 132, 135, 138, 139, 144, 158,
169, 173, 176, 177, 179, 193, 194, 195, 196, 200,
201); **Derek Hillier** (pages 12, 20, 27, 31, 86, 87,
102, 108, 141, 192, 201); **Jojo** (pages 8, 28, 39, 44,
48, 50, 68, 110, 145, 170, 187, 207); **David Hitner**
(pages 11, 13, 65, 67, 74, 85, 106, 115, 140, 159,
162, 163, 165, 183, 198); **Alexia Cox** (pages 30, 46,
83, 88, 128, 148, 157); **Kevin Gould** (pages 13, 107,
130, 190); **Sara Geeves** (pages 141, 183); **Theo Gould**
(page 182); **Luigi Beltrandi** (page 84); **Elisabeth Cox**
(page 41); **Rupert Cox** (page 40); **Noel Murphy** (page
206), courtesy *Waitrose Food Illustrated*.

Illustrations by **Trevor Smith** (pages 7, 102, 162).

Cover – photography **Derek Hillier**,
Kitchen roll manufactured by Goulds (D.M.) Ltd.

Quality Marks (page 112–113),
courtesy Meat and Livestock Commission.

Endpapers – Tiblisi Tablecloth, courtesy Jason Lowe.

Hodder and Stoughton
A division of Hodder Headline
338 Euston Road, London NW1 3BH

KEVIN GOULD

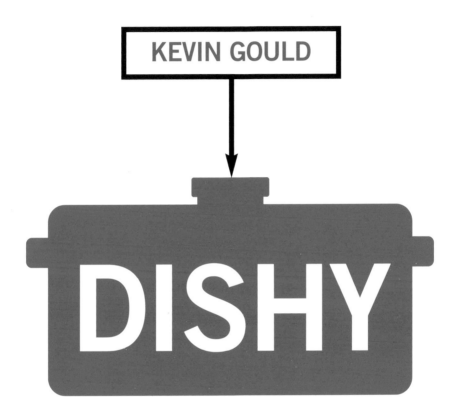

DISHY

Hodder & Stoughton

CONTENTS

THANK YOU FOR CHOOSING DISHY
All **DISHY** writing, graphics and recipes are carefully designed to give you confidence around the kitchen.

DISHY INGREDIENTS

MUSIC
You need to have your favourite sounds in the kitchen. Like your music, **DISHY** cooking is about rhythm, relaxation and emotion. Hearing your beats is going to help you cook with balls, style and enjoyment.

A SUPERMARKET
All of the ingredients in **DISHY**, apart perhaps from fresh truffles and bottarga, which are mentioned twice, are available from any decent supermarket. And there are supermarket alternatives given for truffles and bottarga, anyway, so that's that.

CHOICE SKILLS
You have to choose quality. Quality is not the same as luxury, although there is sensual pleasure in choosing the best ingredients you can find.

You wouldn't choose to go out in a coat that dissolves in the rain, because that would be a waste of money, and you'd get wet. So, for the same reason, you shouldn't choose a rubbish battery chicken if there's a free-range or organic one easily available. Nobody really knows what effect chemicals in food production have on the human body, so choosing ingredients in their most natural state shows that you're interested in looking after number one.

Your body's a machine that needs you to choose quality ingredients (and regular servicing) if it's to give you long-lasting pleasure, so **DISHY** food helps you look after it. You tiger, you.

READING SKILLS
DISHY people get the habit of checking ingredients labels in the supermarket – all the ingredients you need to get hold of shouldn't contain nasty E's. Too many E's can turn you into your parents. Avoid products where the ingredients read like a chemical formula. Most chemicals are put in foods for the convenience of the producer and the supermarket, not for your convenience.

YOU DO NOT NEED ANY KITCHEN EXPERIENCE TO BE DISHY
Preparing dishes and eating well should be a joy and not a chore, so **DISHY** isn't about Home Economics, but it is about sound sense, having a laugh and getting results. Those results include magicking up special dishes for your mates, and helping you to impress that special person.

SELF-RESPECT
Of course you want to put better food inside you, so that you'll stay healthier longer! Of course you want to see dishes through from start to delicious finish! Of course you want to develop new kitchen skills that make you more attractive to other people!

DRESS SENSE
You know your Paul Smith from your Joe Bloggs. Cooking to please uses the same skills as dressing to kill. Choosing colours and clothes is the same as combining flavours and foods.

ATTITUDE
Your positive attitude is essential in the kitchen. You can achieve any and all of these recipes just by following the flowcharts and concentrating on the action.

DISHY doesn't offer serving suggestions with a studio picture of an impossible dish. These are not cookery tests to be marked out of 10: your result is the right result – taste it, it'll be delicious! Gold star.

REALITY
DISHY is Real Food. Real Food is food that hasn't been mucked about with or over-processed in some factory. Real Food is food with integrity, food you can be proud of, and food for your future.

Olives

Serves a groovy party for swingers

GREEN OLIVES
- 300g green olives
- 1 lemon
- 6 mint leaves

BLACK OLIVES
- 1 red chile
- 4 tablespoons of supermarket olive oil
- A handful of coriander leaves
- 1 large clove of garlic
- 300g black olives

See also Potatoes Refried with Olives and Rosemary (page 163), in the Leftover chapter.

IMPORTANT NOTICE

Avoid cheap black olives. Black olives are simply green ones that are left longer to ripen on the tree. In doing so, some fall to the ground, which lose the farmer money. Some brilliant person realised that if the olives were picked unripe, they could be dyed with iron solution and sold as luxury black olives. Apart from any potential health issues, dyed olives taste dull. You can always tell a dyed black olive by the consistent colour: sun-ripened black olives are shades of blacks and browns. Also, dyed olives have black stones where the iron dye has penetrated the flesh.

Olives are a grown-up taste. Olives mean sophistication, élan, chic, but most shop-bought olives just taste salty. So if you're going to buy them, personalise them by adding something hot or cool to show that you possess a certain individual style...

Olives keep for weeks when covered in olive oil... a few leftover olives can be cut up into small bits and thrown into any salad...

Drain the olives and place them in a bowl.

↓

Juice the lemon and add it to the olives.

↓

Shred the mint leaves and stir them into the olives.

↓

Leave to stand for 30–60 minutes before serving.

Remove the seeds from the chile, slice it very finely and place it in a bowl with the olive oil.

↓

WARNING
Wash your hands well after touching the fiery seeds. Don't touch your eyes or your flies.

↓

Chop the coriander leaves and the garlic and stir them into the olive oil.

↓

Leave to stand for at least 1 hour or preferably overnight, covered.

↓

Drain the olives and place them in a bowl.

↓

Pour the aromatic oil over the olives, stir and serve.

↓

Keep in a fridge, in a covered container, for a month, if you have enough discipline.

↓

Bring back to room temperature before serving.

Olive Paste

Serves a groovy party for swingers

GREEN OLIVE PASTE
- 300g green olive paste
- 3 tablespoons of flaked almonds

BLACK OLIVE PASTE
- 300g black olive paste
- 6 cardamom pods
- 2 tablespoons of orange juice

Alternative uses for olive pastes:
- Spread on baguette 'pennies' that you've lightly toasted to turn them into crostini.
- Mix with mayonnaise to serve with salads.
- Spoon over freshly cooked pasta and finish with grated Parmesan.
- Spread thinly on sandwiches instead of butter, or as a sort of grown-up Marmite.

It's worth buying a jar of olive paste – kept in the fridge covered with olive oil, pastes last for months and can save you when there's not much else around to eat. Olive pastes are much of a muchness, unless you find one made form a specific type of olive, that's been hand-crushed between the thighs of novice nuns, or something, so here's a couple of ways of tarting them up to impress your worldly friends.

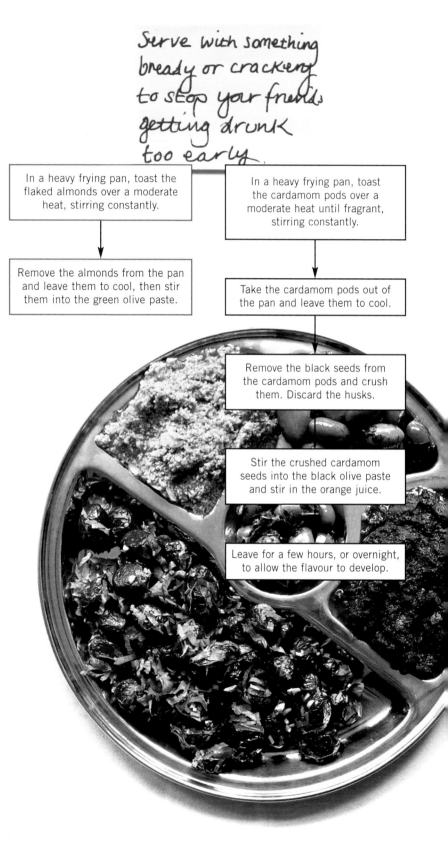

Serve with something bready or crackery to stop your friends getting drunk too early.

In a heavy frying pan, toast the flaked almonds over a moderate heat, stirring constantly.

Remove the almonds from the pan and leave them to cool, then stir them into the green olive paste.

In a heavy frying pan, toast the cardamom pods over a moderate heat until fragrant, stirring constantly.

Take the cardamom pods out of the pan and leave them to cool.

Remove the black seeds from the cardamom pods and crush them. Discard the husks.

Stir the crushed cardamom seeds into the black olive paste and stir in the orange juice.

Leave for a few hours, or overnight, to allow the flavour to develop.

Chargrilled Asparagus with Maldon Sea Salt

Serves 4

- 12 spears of asparagus
  or 24 spears if they're the thin
  spindly type
- Olive oil
- Maldon Sea salt

*Maldon Sea salt is flaky and crystalline.
Its advantage to those of us with great
taste lies in Maldon's less-salty-more-
minerally flavour, and the softness of its
crystals, which crumble in your fingers.*

Cut the asparagus spears
to a uniform size, trimming off
any tough woody ends.

Heat your chargrill until
it's very hot.

Turn the heat down to
medium-low and lay the asparagus
on the chargrill.

Cook for up to 12 minutes,
turning the asparagus so that it
cooks on all sides – you'll know
it's cooked when the sides are
charred a fetching mottled
vibrant-green/dark brown colour,
and when the spears have lost
some of their firmness.
(It happens to us all, in time).

Put some olive oil and salt
in separate bowls and serve with
the asparagus.

Pick up the lovely, charry
asparagus spears by the end
and dip them first into the oil,
then the salt.

This is the easiest, yet maybe
the most stylish thing you
can do with asparagus,
with the added advantage
that there's no oil or butter
used in the cooking to freak
out the fat counters.
Eating asparagus makes
your pee smell like the mild
exciting animal you are.

NO
CHOLESTEROL

Persian Herbs with Feta, Radishes and Flatbread

Serves 4

- 200g feta cheese
- 25g/large handful of basil, preferably purple
- 25g/large handful of mint
- 25g/large handful of tarragon
- 16 radishes
- 16 spring onions
- 4 pieces of flatbread, such as taftoun, naan or pitta

Travellers to the East may hear the Persians say that starting a meal with something fresh and green brings good luck: indeed, they make a point of eating this as the first dish of Now Roozi their New Year, which generally falls in March.

Relax, use your fingers, feel saintly for eating so many raw herbs.... Grab your supermarket managers and tell them you want to see a better selection of fresh ~~herbs~~ herbs sold in bigger... Radish adds colour and crunch, but may make your breath a bit farty: try sweet baby cucumbers, raw red peppers or chunks of carrot for a change.

Break the feta into roughly equal pieces and divide between the serving plates.

Pick over the herbs, chucking out any discoloured leaves, and trim the radishes and spring onions.

Toast the flatbread in a toaster, or under the grill, or warm in the oven.

Arrange the herbs and vegetables on the plates with the cheese and serve with the flatbread.

Roasted Vine Tomato Soup

Mezze Platter

Serves 6 with leftovers

ROASTED SWEET AND HOT PEPPER MUSH
- 4 red bell peppers
- 2 red chiles
- Olive oil
- 2 cloves of garlic

BABA GHANOUJ
- 6 fresh aubergines, or ones that are slightly past it
- About 4 tablespoons of light tahini
- 1 large lemon
- 2 large cloves of garlic
- A splash of olive oil
- Salt

HUMMOUS
- 250g tub of ready-made hummous
- Juice of 1 lemon
- 1 tablespoon of olive oil
- A pinch of paprika or chile powder

Serve with:
- Flatbreads – either taftoun, naan or pitta, stuck in the toaster or under the grill for about 15 seconds
- Sticks of cucumber, or carrot, or celery, or pepper, or all of them
- Leaves of cos lettuce. Why? Cos.

Heat the oven to 200°C/400°F/Gas Mark 6.

Rub the bell peppers and chiles all over with a little olive oil and place them in a roasting tin. Peel the garlic cloves and add them to the tin.

Roast for 20 minutes or until the skins of the bell peppers are blackened, turning halfway through cooking. If the chiles blacken faster than the peppers, remove them from the oven and continue to roast the peppers.

To peel the skins easily, place the peppers and chiles in a plastic bag, tie a loose knot in the end, and set aside for 15 minutes.

Core, peel and deseed the peppers and the chile (leave the seeds in the chile if you like spicy food). Keep any cooking juices to add to the mush.

Either
Place the peppers in a food processor with the roasted garlic and pulse until relatively smooth, adding just enough olive oil to make a paste.

Or
Place the peppers in a bowl with the roasted garlic and mash with a fork until relatively smooth, adding just enough olive oil to make a paste.

Serve in a bowl, wearing dark denim.

BABA GHANOUJ

IS THE LEAST BORING ARABIC WAY OF SAYING 'GRILLED AUBERGINES MASHED WITH A BIT OF SESAME PASTE'. A GOOD WAY OF IMPRESSING WORLDLY PALS IS TO PRONOUNCE 'BABA GHANOUJ' IN THE AUTHENTIC ARAB STYLE, AS IF YOU'RE A CANDIDATE FOR MAJOR THROAT SURGERY. FURTHER POINTS CAN BE GAINED FOR EXPLAINING THAT IN LEBANON, THE DRUZE OFTEN CALL THIS DISH 'MOUTABAL'. THINK OF THREE INVENTIVE REASONS WHY THAT MIGHT BE, AND CROSS GO.

Stick a fork in the end of each aubergine and rotate each one over the naked flame of a gas hob (or fire) until thoroughly charred. Alternatively, char them under a hot grill.

↓

Place the tahini in a small bowl and squeeze the juice from the lemon into the tahini. Beat the bejasus out of the mixture: it will go stiff at first but keep going until it turns thin enough to pour.

↓

Remove the charred aubergines from the heat and leave them to cool for about 10 minutes.

↓

Peel the garlic and squash the cloves with the flat end of a knife to break them up.

↓

When the aubergines are cool, peel off the skin and place the flesh in a large bowl. Mash with a fork, then add the garlic and keep mashing to a lumpy consistency.

↓

Beat the tahini and lemon mixture into the aubergine until well incorporated.

↓

Add a good splash of olive oil and keep beating for about a minute, or until your arm hurts.

↓

Taste and add salt if you think it needs it.

Beat the lemon juice into the hummous with a fork until it's disappeared.

↓

Put the hummous on a serving dish, and make a little well in the middle.

↓

Pour in the slug of olive oil.

↓

Taste it. Does it taste good? Does it need more salt?

↓

Sprinkle the paprika over the top, or make designs based on lines or diamonds – or your name, if you're that type of person.

A little hand-to-mouth action causes small pauses in conversations and breaks the ice in new situations....
Hummous is easy but slow to make, so buy it in and dress it up.

Prosciutto and Salame with Figs

Serves 4

- 8 small fresh sexy figs
  or 4 large ones
- 12 thin slices of charcuterie, such
  as Parma or Serrano ham, spicy
  chorizo, Felino or Milano salame
- 2 green olives (if you like olives)
- Black pepper

Using a small sharp knife, make a cross by the stem of each fig.

↓

Gently stick your finger through the cross in each fig and wiggle it about a bit.

↓

Ruffle up a slice of meat and insert it in a fig so that it looks like it's erupting like a plume. Repeat with the remaining meat and figs.

↓

Grind black pepper over the top and garnish each fig with a sliver of green olive, if olives are your thing.

↓

Serve 1 large or 2 small figs per person on separate serving plates. Alternatively, arrange them all on a platter for guests to choose their own.

Alternatively

If fresh figs aren't available, wrap a slice of Parma or Serrano ham around the end of 12 breadsticks and eat like a savoury lolly.

Fresh figs are sexy. They're curvy and smooth, and when cut they reveal fleshy skin and intimate seeds whose secret is that they need no help to fertilise themselves

Figs might remind you of those perfectly self-contained attractive people, well aware of and comfortable with their sexuality, and desired by nearly everyone.... pushing in salami or raw Parma ham kind of completes the picture.

KEVIN GOULD

Buffalo Mozzarella with Charred Cherry Tomatoes

Serves 4

- About 6 large basil leaves
- Olive oil
- 12 cherry tomatoes
- A handful of rocket or spinach leaves
- 4 balls of buffalo mozzarella cheese, or a plait
- 1 tablespoon of red wine vinegar
- Salt and black pepper

Tear up the basil leaves and place them in a small bowl with 3 tablespoons of olive oil. Leave to stand for at least 30 minutes.

Just before serving, heat a chargrill or overhead grill until very hot.

Cut the tomatoes in half widthways.

Place a tablespoon of olive oil in a small bowl and throw in a pinch of salt and black pepper.

Dip the cut ends of the tomatoes in the seasoned olive oil and place them cut-end down on the chargrill or below the overhead grill – not too close or they're charcoal. Cook for 1–2 minutes until browned.

Arrange the cherry tomatoes charred-side up around the cheese.

Add the red wine vinegar to the remaining basil oil and whisk with a fork until it's nicely blended. Drizzle this mixture around the plates.

Grind black pepper over the top – asking the lady if she likes it hot and spicy? – and serve.

Arrange a handful of rocket or spinach leaves on each serving plate.

Slice the mozzarella and divide it among the plates.

Spoon a little of the basil oil around each plate.

Quality Smoked Salmon with Cos Lettuce, Caperberries and Fresh Limes

👤👤👤👤

Serves 4

- ½ lime
- 200g slices of wild smoked salmon
- A handful of caperberries
- Black pepper

OPTION
- About 12 small leaves of a cos lettuce, or a little gem (if you like)

Squeeze the juice from the lime and season to taste with freshly ground black pepper. Place it in a mister (see page 121).

Using the mister, spritz the salmon lightly with the lime juice and arrange on serving plates.

Option

Place a slice of smoked salmon inside each lettuce leaf – if you're into the lettuce. Using the mister, spritz the lettuce and salmon lightly with the lime juice and arrange on serving plates.

Garnish with the caperberries and tell your posse that you're getting jiggy with it.

IMPORTANT NOTICE

Avoid the cheapo smoked salmon if you can – it's almost guaranteed to be greasy, dyed crap. Many of the farmed fish lead awful lives, and are fed a daily diet of antibiotics, anti-fungals and E numbers to colour them pink. A real salmon's normal diet includes tiny shellfish, which pink them up nicely, and lots of exercise, which keeps them lean. Most fish farms find that their salmon are so crammed into cages, and get so flabby as a result that they have to be starved for two or three days before being lifted. Otherwise, when they're smoked, they drop up to five litres of oil per fish, an inconvenience that puts out the smoking fires and makes the salmon taste like hand cream…

Real wild salmon is increasingly rare and very expensive. It tastes kind of gamier than the farmed variety, and costs kind of ten times the price. Lottery winners should apply to Harrods Food Hall, where they should ask for a side of Mr Forman's best wild, two dozen Belon oysters, and some vinegar for the inevitable chip on their shoulder. Salmon 'ranched' in Scottish sea lochs is a good sub-stitute, especially if they've been fed organic food.

Capers are flower buds that grow against walls in hot, sunny countries. They're usually pickled in brine or vinegar and left on the side of finished pizzas, together with the chewy, burnt crusts.

Caperberries grow if the bud of the caper is not picked, and the resultant flower is fertilised. Caperberries taste more subtle than capers, and their interesting shape and texture makes them useful as a kind of posh olive.

Roasted Vine Tomato Soup

Serves 4

- 1.5kg vine tomatoes
- Olive oil
- 1 head of garlic
- A large knob of butter
- Salt and black pepper
- A few basil leaves
  if you fancy

Heat the oven to
150°C/300°F/Gas Mark 2.

Rub the tomatoes with olive oil
and place them in a roasting tin with
the whole head of garlic.

Roast for up to 1½ hours until the
tomatoes are nicely shrivelled but not
browned. Check the garlic from time to
time, and if the top goes darker than
caramel colour, remove from the oven.

If you make soup, you're seen as a home-
maker, which is sometimes no bad thing. If
you make roasted vine-tomato soup, you'll
be seen as the type of home-maker who
skims through wallpaper and knows their
Prada from their C&A.

Remove from the oven and leave
until just cool enough to handle.

Meanwhile, boil some water.

Slip off and discard the
tomato skins and place the tomatoes
in a large saucepan.

Snip the top off the garlic
bulb and squeeze the soft interior
into a small bowl.

Set the pan over a low heat
and add a large knob of butter.

Mash the roasted garlic paste
until smooth, adding a pinch of
salt to help turn it into a cream.

Using a wooden spoon, squeeze the
tomatoes against the side of the pan
until the mixture turns into soup.

Remind your friends that you prefer vine
tomatoes because they've matured longer
on the vine and therefore tend to be
sweeter, have a fuller flavour than the
regular red bullets, and also that you never
store your tomatoes in the fridge as it stops
them tasting ripe.

Add some shredded fresh
basil leaves to the soup if
you fancy.

Add some boiled water to the soup
to thin it to pouring consistency
– you should have about 1.2 litres
if you can be arsed to measure it.

Taste the soup – it should taste sweetly
of tomatoes, and add salt as necessary.

Discuss Disney movies
and the marketing merits
(or otherwise) of calling
a film *Free Willy*.

Serve the soup with a small dollop
of the garlic cream in each bowl.

Prosciutto and Salame with Figs

Chargrilled Asparagus with Maldon Sea Salt

Fish Soup with her Rouille

👤👤👤👤

Serves 4

- 12 unopened scallops
- 12 large raw prawns
- 450g firm white fish such as dabs,
  ling, sole or whiting
- 450g monkfish, about 1 large
  monkfish tail or 2 small tails
- 600ml mussels
- 600ml clams
- 4 slices of stale bread
- A pinch of saffron threads
- 300ml single cream
- 4 tablespoons of red pepper paste,
  red pesto, rouille or black olive paste
- Grated Parmesan or Gruyère cheese
- Salt and black pepper

TIME TO BURN
- 1 white onion or 3–4 shallots
- A knob of butter
- 6 peppercorns
- 1 bay leaf

NO TIME TO LOSE
- 1.2 litres of shop-bought fish stock

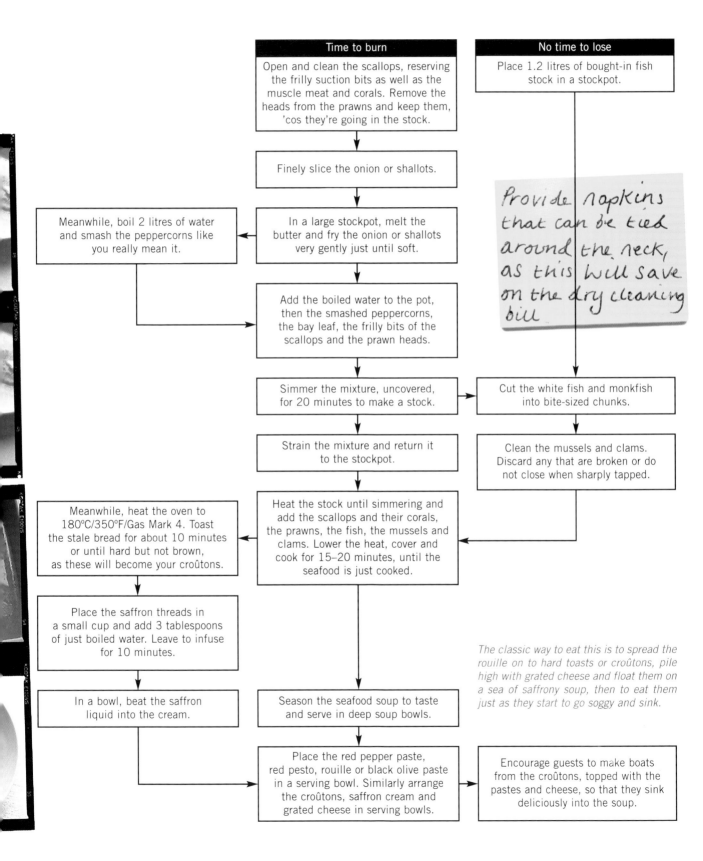

Time to burn	No time to lose
Open and clean the scallops, reserving the frilly suction bits as well as the muscle meat and corals. Remove the heads from the prawns and keep them, 'cos they're going in the stock.	Place 1.2 litres of bought-in fish stock in a stockpot.

Finely slice the onion or shallots.

Provide napkins that can be tied around the neck, as this will save on the dry cleaning bill

Meanwhile, boil 2 litres of water and smash the peppercorns like you really mean it. → In a large stockpot, melt the butter and fry the onion or shallots very gently just until soft.

Add the boiled water to the pot, then the smashed peppercorns, the bay leaf, the frilly bits of the scallops and the prawn heads.

Simmer the mixture, uncovered, for 20 minutes to make a stock. → Cut the white fish and monkfish into bite-sized chunks.

Strain the mixture and return it to the stockpot. | Clean the mussels and clams. Discard any that are broken or do not close when sharply tapped.

Meanwhile, heat the oven to 180°C/350°F/Gas Mark 4. Toast the stale bread for about 10 minutes or until hard but not brown, as these will become your croûtons. ← Heat the stock until simmering and add the scallops and their corals, the prawns, the fish, the mussels and clams. Lower the heat, cover and cook for 15–20 minutes, until the seafood is just cooked.

Place the saffron threads in a small cup and add 3 tablespoons of just boiled water. Leave to infuse for 10 minutes.

The classic way to eat this is to spread the rouille on to hard toasts or croûtons, pile high with grated cheese and float them on a sea of saffrony soup, then to eat them just as they start to go soggy and sink.

In a bowl, beat the saffron liquid into the cream. | Season the seafood soup to taste and serve in deep soup bowls.

Place the red pepper paste, red pesto, rouille or black olive paste in a serving bowl. Similarly arrange the croûtons, saffron cream and grated cheese in serving bowls. → Encourage guests to make boats from the croûtons, topped with the pastes and cheese, so that they sink deliciously into the soup.

Tortellini in Brodo

👤👤👤👤

Serves 4

- 1.2 litres of beef or chicken stock
  (see page 153)
  or 1.2 litres of vegetable stock
  (see page 152)
- 20 little beef tortellini
  or 12 large beef tortelloni
  or 20 ricotta and spinach tortellini
  or 12 ricotta and spinach tortelloni
- A few chives, basil leaves, rocket
  or wild garlic, depending on the
  time of year
- Salt and black pepper
- Grated Parmesan

1) A great way to make a little filled pasta go a long way by serving it in a clear broth.

2) A dish that reminds you of that wonderful lunch at the Montegrappa da Nello near the Piazza Nettuno in Bologna, famous for its local prosciutto and Tortellini in Brodo.

Heat the stock in a large saucepan until it's on a rolling boil. Add the pasta, and cook it for as long as it says on the packet.

↓

Taste it. Does it taste good? Does it need salt?

↓

Divide the pasta and stock into serving bowls.

↓

Snip the herbs over the top.

↓

Offer fresh grated Parmesan to sprinkle liberally over the soup.

Tortellini are small, Tortelloni are big. Tortellini are small, Tortelloni are big. Tortellini are small, Tortelloni are big. Tortellini are small, Tortelloni are big. Tortellini are small, Tortelloni are big. Tortellini are small, Tortelloni are big. Tortellini are small, Tortelloni are big. Tortellini are small, Tortelloni are big. Tortellini are small, Tortelloni are big. Tortellini are small, Tortelloni are big. Tortellini are small, Tortelloni are big. Tortellini are small, Tortelloni are big. Tortellini are small, Tortelloni are big. Tortellini are small, Tortelloni are big. Tortellini are small, Tortelloni are big. Tortellini are small, Tortelloni are big.

Egyptian Bread Soup

ŤŤŤŤ/ŤŤŤŤŤŤ

Serves 4–6

- 1 tablespoon of olive oil
- 1 large onion
- 1kg fresh or frozen mixed vegetables such as green beans, cabbage, carrots, celeriac, spinach or swede
- 400g canned borlotti beans or ful mesdames
- ½ teaspoon of dried thyme
- 1 teaspoon of cumin seeds
- 1 handful of hazelnuts
- 4 slices of stale bread
- Salt and black pepper

The national dish in Egypt is molokchia, named after the leafy green vegetable that grows along the shores of the Nile. When cooked, molokchia turns into a phlegmy green sludge. Egyptians say they love it, but you might think they're just in denial.

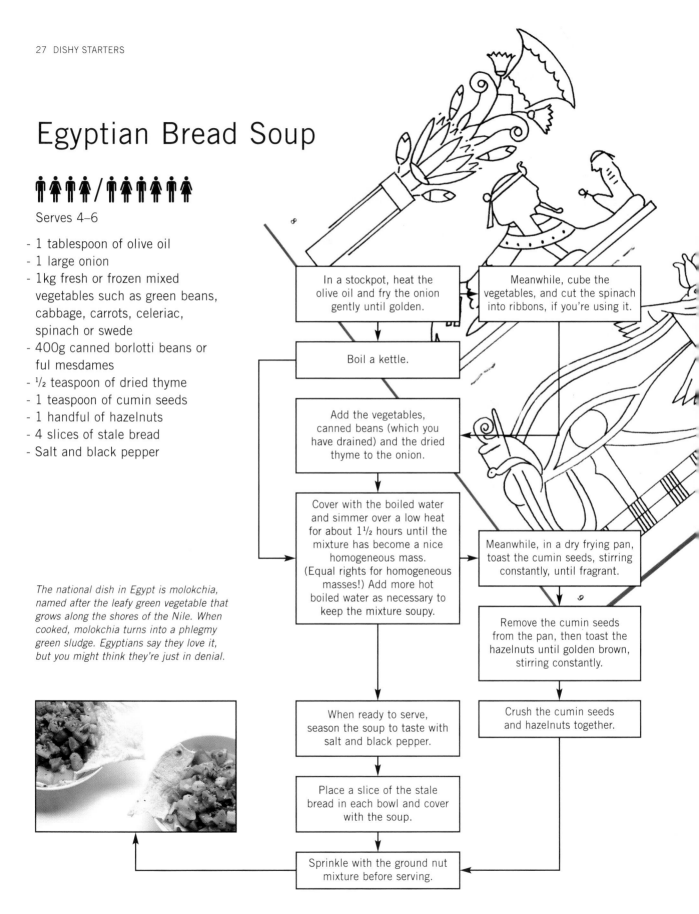

In a stockpot, heat the olive oil and fry the onion gently until golden.

Meanwhile, cube the vegetables, and cut the spinach into ribbons, if you're using it.

Boil a kettle.

Add the vegetables, canned beans (which you have drained) and the dried thyme to the onion.

Cover with the boiled water and simmer over a low heat for about 1½ hours until the mixture has become a nice homogeneous mass. (Equal rights for homogeneous masses!) Add more hot boiled water as necessary to keep the mixture soupy.

Meanwhile, in a dry frying pan, toast the cumin seeds, stirring constantly, until fragrant.

Remove the cumin seeds from the pan, then toast the hazelnuts until golden brown, stirring constantly.

When ready to serve, season the soup to taste with salt and black pepper.

Crush the cumin seeds and hazelnuts together.

Place a slice of the stale bread in each bowl and cover with the soup.

Sprinkle with the ground nut mixture before serving.

Simple Leaf Salad with Vinaigrette

Serves 2 as a light snack with some cheese and bread, or 4 as a side salad

- 80–100g bag of ready-washed mixed salad leaves
- A handful of fresh herb leaves, such as basil, chervil, coriander, dill or parsley
- 2–3 tablespoons of olive oil
- A squeeze of lemon juice or a splash of your favourite vinegar
- Salt

OPTION
- A heaped teaspoon of your favourite mustard

Rinse the salad leaves and leave them to drain in a colander, shaking them a few times as necessary.

↓

Place the salad leaves in a large bowl with the herbs.

↓

Add the oil, lemon juice and salt to taste.

↓

Toss and serve, smile and wave, smile and wave.

Option
Mix the lemon juice or vinegar into the mustard, then pour in the olive oil, stirring the whole while. Taste the vinaigrette to see if you think it needs salt.

Buying a bag of ready-washed salad leaves and tarting them up with some fresh herbs is a dishy thing to do, as it shows that you're busy, creative, practical and chic.

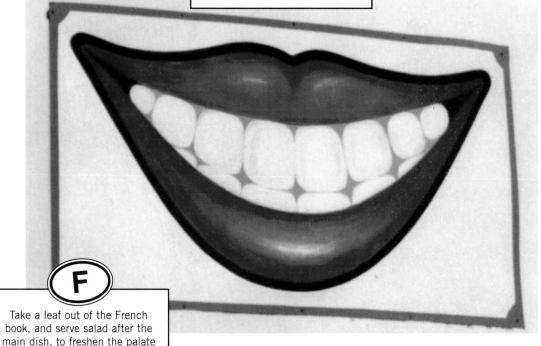

(F)
Take a leaf out of the French book, and serve salad after the main dish, to freshen the palate and buy time before dessert.

Provençal Fennel

👨‍👩 / 👨‍👩‍👧‍👧

Serves 2–4

- 1 fennel bulb
- 1 onion
- 1 tablespoon of olive oil
- 400g canned tomatoes
- A few peppercorns
- ½ teaspoon of fresh oregano
- 1 bay leaf
- A pinch of dried basil
- Salt
- Wire bouquet garni ball or a small square of muslin

Provence has been so 'discovered' as to appear more like the 'Provençal Experience' than the enchanting region it is.
Provence has one of the kindest climates in the world, and scented, romantic air that makes you feel like listening to Sacha Distel records and drinking unwise quantities of wine.

Trim the base off the fennel, then cut it lengthways into batons just a bit thicker than a matchstick, reserving the attractive fennel fronds to use as a garnish.

⬇

Slice the onion. Heat the olive oil in a medium saucepan, add the onion and cook over a low heat until soft but not coloured, stirring occasionally. Add the fennel and cook for 1 minute.

⬇

Stir in the tomatoes, squeezing them against the inside of the pan with the back of a wooden spoon.

This is very delicious, particularly when eaten in Provence. It also goes very well with Roast Lamb (see page 117) or Lamb Cutlets (see page 129).

Either
Bruise the peppercorns and add them to the mixture along with the herbs.

Or
Bruise the peppercorns. Place them with the herbs in a wire bouquet garni ball or a muslin bag and add them to the mixture.

Taste it. Does it need salt?

⬇

Simmer over a low heat, stirring and squashing the mixture regularly, for 15–20 minutes, or a bit longer – the longer you cook it, the less crunchy the vegetables and the thicker the sauce.

Serving Option A
Serve garnished with the fennel fronds.

Serving Option B
Remove the bouquet garni and serve, garnished with the fennel fronds.

Standby Lemon Chickpeas

Serves 2–4 after an evening's drinking

- 1 large onion
- 5 tablespoons of olive oil
- 400g canned chickpeas
- 1 lemon
- Salt and black pepper

Chickpea to Cook

A chickpea leaps almost over the rim of the pot
where it's being boiled.

"Why are you doing this to me?"

The cook knocks him down with the ladle.

"Don't you try to jump out.
You think I'm torturing you.
I'm giving you flavor,
so you can mix with spices and rice
and be the lovely vitality of a human being.

Remember when you drank rain in the garden.
That was for this."

Grace first. Sexual pleasure,
then a boiling new life begins,
and the Friend has something good to eat.

Eventually the chickpea
will say to the cook,
                "Boil me some more.
Hit me with the skimming spoon.
I can't do this by myself.

I'm like an elephant that dreams of gardens
back in Hindustan and doesn't pay attention
to his driver. You're my Cook, my Driver,

138

my Way into Existence. I love your cooking."

The Cook says,
                "I was once like you,
fresh from the ground. Then I boiled in Time,
and boiled in the Body, two fierce boilings.

My animal-soul grew powerful.
I controlled it with practices,
and boiled some more, and boiled
once beyond that,
                and became your Teacher."

(*Mathnawi*, III, 4160-4168, 4197-4208)

Flowchart:

Halve the onion horizontally. Chop one half of it and finely slice the other half into rings.

↓

Heat 3 tablespoons of olive oil in a small frying pan and fry the sliced onion rings over a medium heat until brown and crisp. Remove the onions from the pan and drain on kitchen paper.

↓

In a separate pan, heat 2 tablespoons of olive oil and gently fry the chopped onions until soft and golden.

↓

Rinse and drain the chickpeas and add them to the chopped onions. Juice the lemon and add it too. If it all looks too dry for your taste, or if it's catching and burning a bit on the bottom of the pan, add water by the half-teacup 'til you like it better.

↓

Cook for 10 minutes, then taste and add salt and black pepper as desired.

↓

Serve hot or at room temperature, topped with the crispy onion rings.

Double or triple the ingredients. This dish tastes great, and may even taste better when it's been in the fridge for 4 or 5 days, ready for when you come in wrecked late at night, needing something munchy and savoury to eat and that's undemanding to put together.

Rumi, the Mathnawi, 3, translated by Coleman Barks, *Delicious Laughter*, Maypop Books, 1990.

Sort of German Marinated Potato Salad with Red Onion Dressing

Serves 4

- 1kg small, waxy potatoes
- 1 large red onion
- 8 tablespoons of olive oil
- About 5 tablespoons of white wine vinegar
- Salt

Rub clean the skins of the potatoes then place them in a large saucepan with water to cover. Bring to the boil and simmer for 15–20 minutes, or until almost tender. Drain the potatoes and leave them until cool enough to handle.

Meanwhile, quarter the onion and smack each wedge with the heel of a large knife to release the juices and make the onions crunchier. Chop the onion finely, reserving a few slices to use as a garnish.

Throw 3 tablespoons of olive oil into a small bowl and flavour it with a generous sprinkling of salt. Halve the potatoes lengthways, then dip the cut side into the salty oil.

Heat a griddle or heavy frying pan until very hot. Place the potatoes cut-side down on the surface and sear them until nicely browned, without turning.

Transfer the seared potatoes to the salad bowl, stir to combine, then cover and store in the fridge for 2 days.

Place the chopped onion in a deep Tupperware or Pyrex bowl with 5 tablespoons of olive oil and 5 tablespoons of vinegar.

Serve the salad with lots of the dressing or, if you prefer, drained a little. Garnish with the reserved slices of onion, which will have bleached slightly while in the fridge.

Place the slices of onion in a small bowl, splash them with a little vinegar and store in the refrigerator until needed.

Holds well in hot weather, so it's perfect for picnics, but it's equally gratifying anytime, especially when accompanied with a big glass of cold lager ...

Think Franz Beckenbauer, think Steffi Graf, think Ferdinand Porsche, think Braun, think Green. That's enough thinking, now eat.

Baked Potatoes with Pesto and Other Things

Serves 4

- 4 baking potatoes
- Olive oil
- Maldon Sea salt
- 1 teaspoon of chile powder
  (if you fancy)

For the toppings:
- 150g fresh basil pesto and
  a few pine nuts
- or 4 large knobs of butter and
  a little cream
- or 400–500g cottage cheese
  and a few tarragon leaves

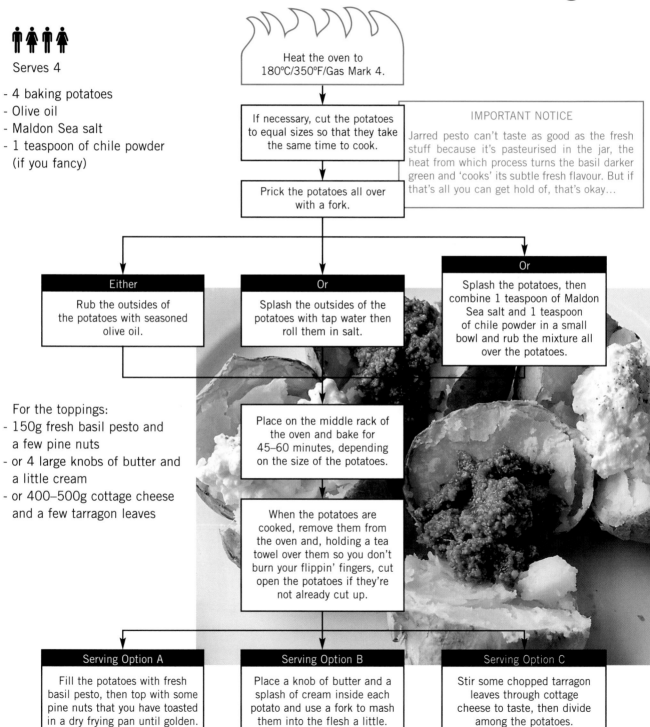

Heat the oven to
180°C/350°F/Gas Mark 4.

If necessary, cut the potatoes
to equal sizes so that they take
the same time to cook.

IMPORTANT NOTICE

Jarred pesto can't taste as good as the fresh
stuff because it's pasteurised in the jar, the
heat from which process turns the basil darker
green and 'cooks' its subtle fresh flavour. But if
that's all you can get hold of, that's okay…

Prick the potatoes all over
with a fork.

Either

Rub the outsides of
the potatoes with seasoned
olive oil.

Or

Splash the outsides of the
potatoes with tap water then
roll them in salt.

Or

Splash the potatoes, then
combine 1 teaspoon of Maldon
Sea salt and 1 teaspoon
of chile powder in a small
bowl and rub the mixture all
over the potatoes.

Place on the middle rack of
the oven and bake for
45–60 minutes, depending
on the size of the potatoes.

When the potatoes are
cooked, remove them from
the oven and, holding a tea
towel over them so you don't
burn your flippin' fingers, cut
open the potatoes if they're
not already cut up.

Serving Option A

Fill the potatoes with fresh
basil pesto, then top with some
pine nuts that you have toasted
in a dry frying pan until golden.

Serving Option B

Place a knob of butter and a
splash of cream inside each
potato and use a fork to mash
them into the flesh a little.

Serving Option C

Stir some chopped tarragon
leaves through cottage
cheese to taste, then divide
among the potatoes.

Bitter Leaves and Caramelised Shallots with Apple Dressing

Serves 4

- 8 shallots (200g)
- Olive oil
- About 1 tablespoon of brown sugar, or honey
- 1 green apple
- 250g bitter salad leaves, such as radicchio, or rocket, or watercress, or witloof, or a mixture
- 2 tablespoons of cider vinegar
- Salt

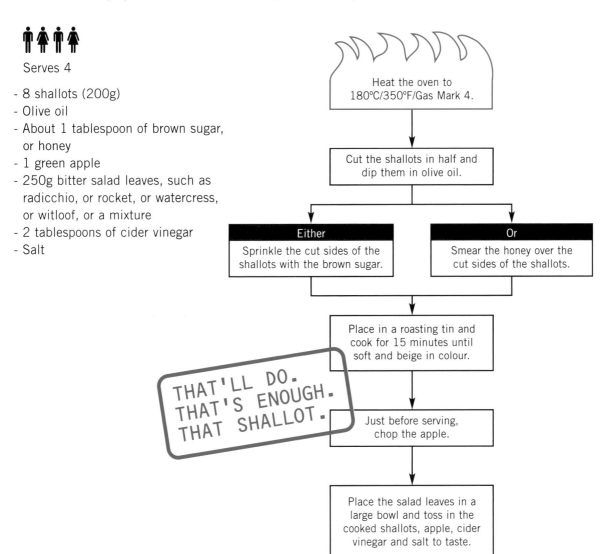

Heat the oven to 180°C/350°F/Gas Mark 4.

Cut the shallots in half and dip them in olive oil.

Either
Sprinkle the cut sides of the shallots with the brown sugar.

Or
Smear the honey over the cut sides of the shallots.

Place in a roasting tin and cook for 15 minutes until soft and beige in colour.

Just before serving, chop the apple.

Place the salad leaves in a large bowl and toss in the cooked shallots, apple, cider vinegar and salt to taste.

THAT'LL DO.
THAT'S ENOUGH.
THAT SHALLOT.

Simple Leaf Salad with Vinaigrette

Grated Carrot, Pine Nut and Orange Blossom Salad

Serves 2–4

- 175g (2 medium-sized) carrots
- ½ orange
- A splash of lemon juice
  (if you like a bit of tartness)
- 1 teaspoon of orange blossom
  water
- 10g pine nuts
- Salt

Orange blossom water, sometimes called orange flower water, is found in most Indian, Cypriot and North African shops. And to make life easier, any good pharmacist either stocks it or can get it tomorrow for you. Orange blossom water makes a wonderful skin cleanser and can also be offered to your friends after a meal for them to wash their fingers in.

Grate the carrots and place them in a bowl.

Juice the orange and add it to the carrots, with a little lemon juice for sharpness if you fancy. Stir in the orange blossom water and a sprinkle of salt.
Leave for 1 hour at room temperature.

Meanwhile, heat up a dry frying pan and toast the pine nuts, stirring constantly, until golden and fragrant. Leave them on a plate to cool.

Just before serving, stir the toasted pine nuts into the carrot mixture. This is a sexy, juicy mixture that needs to be served in a bowl.

PETAL PUSHER

Kevin ... of the bathroom and int...

I lo...
are...
Me...
ba...
gro...
without ha...
water? No ... explains why most flower water in this country is sold at the cosmetic counter, which admits little of the usefulness of scented water in real food.

Making a ...
patience, a ...
Arabic as El ...
her way around Menzel Bouzelfa's blossom festival in northern Tunisia every April, scoring kilos of white rose petals and fragrant orange blossom with which to feed El ...
binding, with ...
the town s...
ed by the l...
back home...
ls her two...
er in the b...
the fragrant water seeps from the spout. Drop by drop, it is ... l the oily surface is ...

My favourite recent acquisition
... water, to be
...rage flower tea

...om orange blossom and roses. But ...ecialises in geranium water. It's not / women, for some reason) tramping ... huge bundles of scented geraniums, ... French colonists called un paradis des ... promised, in hot water taken before ... Mongia is 18 again. Along the same ...ée' (which actually has nothing to do ...ng a teaspoonful to sweetened boiling ... this to our kids before bed and it ...pted sleep.

In Morocco, a salad of grated carrots ... oil and lemon juice, then liberally dous... water. Finished with toasted pine nuts an... segments, this is the kind of dish that ... the 'secret' ingredient. Next time you ... fraiche over your pudding, try flattering it... water beforehand – and be transported. ... elegantly romantic when filled with chunk... with orange flower water. Be flamboy... and harem pants while anointing your gue... from a silver censer!

Into Asia Minor. For at least 5,000 years,... orange blossom water in the kitchen wit... finishes her *khoresh* (a meat stew often w... with apricots, or chicken with pomegra... poonful of the stuff before serving. She als... ummer afternoon with grated apples wh... emon juice, sugar and two tablespoons o... ower water. Humble fruit salad is elevate... mple rice pudding becomes complex and ... ick is to splash a spoonful over really goo... then to throw a cup of espresso coffee over ...

they won't f...
Your avera...
will splash an...
into refreshin...
during the su...
will finish ri...
water. My fav...
sition was pussy willow water, to be drun...
flower tea. This is recommended either ...
decreasing libido, I'm not sure which.

After dinner, Arabic coffee is made mysteri... two of orange flower water. Accompany this w... balls and you're on to a sure thing. For these... sour apricots are minced and sugared, then n... slug of rose water, rolled into marble-sized ... These slightly sharp sweetmeats harmonise de... smoky, syrupy coffee, and are best served f... directly into your partner's mouth.

Butter Baked Witloof

Serves 4

- 40g butter
- 4 witloof
- Salt and black pepper

Heat the oven to 200°C/400°F/Gas Mark 6. Smear butter over the sides and base of a lidded ovenproof casserole dish and dice the remaining butter.

Trim the base of the witloof and remove any browning or wilting leaves. Cut each witloof lengthways into 8 wedges.

Place a layer of witloof on the bottom of the casserole then dot it with some of the diced butter. Repeat until you have used all the witloof and butter.

Sprinkle the casserole with a little salt (or not at all if the butter is salted), then grind over some black pepper.

Cover and cook at the bottom of the oven for 20 minutes without removing the lid. When cooked, the witloof will be shrunk and shrivelled but its flavour will have intensified and there will be delicious caramelised bits on the side and bottom of the dish.

There's a sad, on-going debate as to what this delightful vegetable should be called. Some try chicory, others use endive. Most of it comes from Belgium, where much witloof (white leaf) is cultivated.

The paleness of the leaves is achieved by 'blanching' — essentially stopping the light from reaching the vegetable, either by banking earth over the sprouting leaves or (like mushrooms) growing it in the dark. Without this method, witloof would be much more butter, and the leaves bright green and tough. As we get it, witloof has a pleasing bitterness that is both accentuated and tempered in cooking this never-fail recipe.

☐ WITLOOF
☐ CHICORY
☐ ENDIVE

Pumpkin Stew

Serves 4

- 1 pumpkin, about the size of a football, or 4 small pumpkins
- 2 tablespoons of olive oil
- 1 large onion
- 300ml vegetable stock (see page 152)
- Salt and black pepper

OPTION A
- 6 tablespoons of flaked almonds and 3 tablespoons of crème fraîche

OPTION B
- 500g minced lamb and 6 tablespoons of pine nuts

OPTION C
- Up to 2 mugs of leftover burghul or rice

Pumpkins. Perfect, interesting textures..... blah, blah, blah.... Lots of different varieties... Last for months in the larder... blahdiblahdiblah....

Americans like pumpkins because they remind them of their native Amerindian ancestors, who lived on pumpkins, wild turkey, sweetcorn and fat-reduced-peanut-butter-and-Jello-sandwiches. The French like pumpkins because they're curved like the buttocks of a well-serviced widow. The Italians like pumpkins because they're called zucca, which sounds either like a compliment or an insult, depending on the mood they're in. We like pumpkins because they taste comforting, like grown-up nursery food, and because they look so funky when displayed in a bowl.

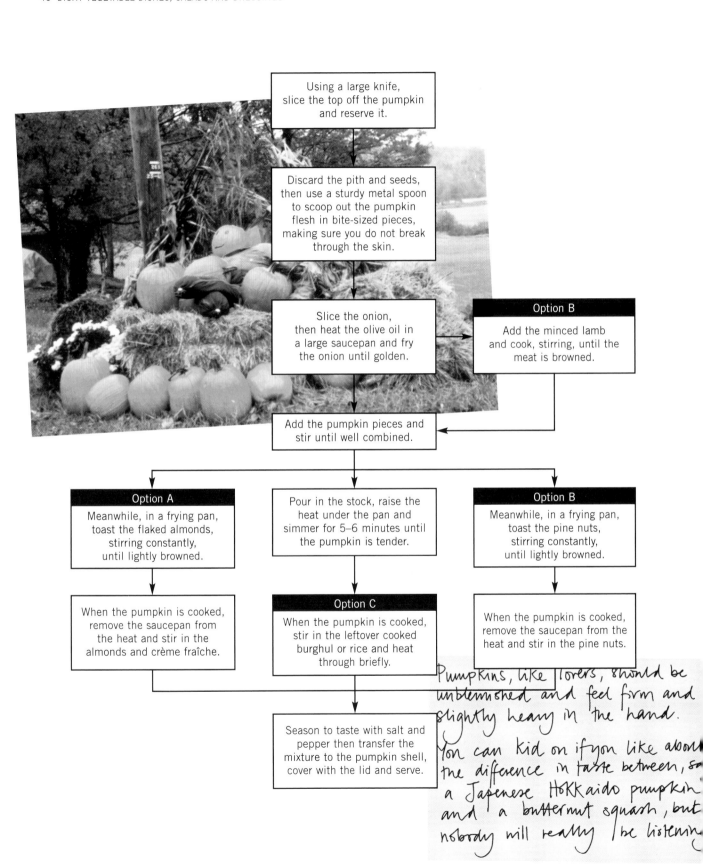

Using a large knife,
slice the top off the pumpkin
and reserve it.

Discard the pith and seeds,
then use a sturdy metal spoon
to scoop out the pumpkin
flesh in bite-sized pieces,
making sure you do not break
through the skin.

Slice the onion,
then heat the olive oil in
a large saucepan and fry
the onion until golden.

Option B

Add the minced lamb
and cook, stirring, until the
meat is browned.

Add the pumpkin pieces and
stir until well combined.

Option A

Meanwhile, in a frying pan,
toast the flaked almonds,
stirring constantly,
until lightly browned.

Pour in the stock, raise the
heat under the pan and
simmer for 5–6 minutes until
the pumpkin is tender.

Option B

Meanwhile, in a frying pan,
toast the pine nuts,
stirring constantly,
until lightly browned.

When the pumpkin is cooked,
remove the saucepan from
the heat and stir in the
almonds and crème fraîche.

Option C

When the pumpkin is cooked,
stir in the leftover cooked
burghul or rice and heat
through briefly.

When the pumpkin is cooked,
remove the saucepan from the
heat and stir in the pine nuts.

Season to taste with salt and
pepper then transfer the
mixture to the pumpkin shell,
cover with the lid and serve.

Pumpkins, like lovers, should be
unblemished and feel firm and
slightly heavy in the hand.

You can kid on if you like about
the difference in taste between, say
a Japanese Hokkaido pumpkin
and a butternut squash, but
nobody will really be listening.

Pumpkin Stew

Porcini Mushrooms

Serves 4

- About 400g fresh porcini
- A knob of butter
- A splash of olive oil
- 2 cloves of garlic
- A few sprigs of parsley
- Salt and black pepper

Boil some water.

Meanwhile, finely chop the parsley.

Place the porcini in the sink and splash about a spoonful of boiling water over each mushroom to drive out any hidden bugs.

Gently melt the butter in a frying pan with a splash of oil and the garlic, until the butter foams.

Pat the mushrooms dry with kitchen paper then slice them lengthways and trim any spongy patches.

Remove the garlic from the pan, then raise the heat and add the mushrooms.

Cook, stirring frequently, just until the mushrooms release their juices and begin to flop – this won't take more than a couple of minutes, and may take even less time than that. You've spent good money on these mushrooms, so protect your investment and don't take your eyes off them for a minute.

When the mushrooms are cooked, season to taste with salt and pepper and stir in the parsley.

Serving Option A

Serve hot by themselves…

Serving Option B

Serve on toast with a glass of wine and a warm friend.

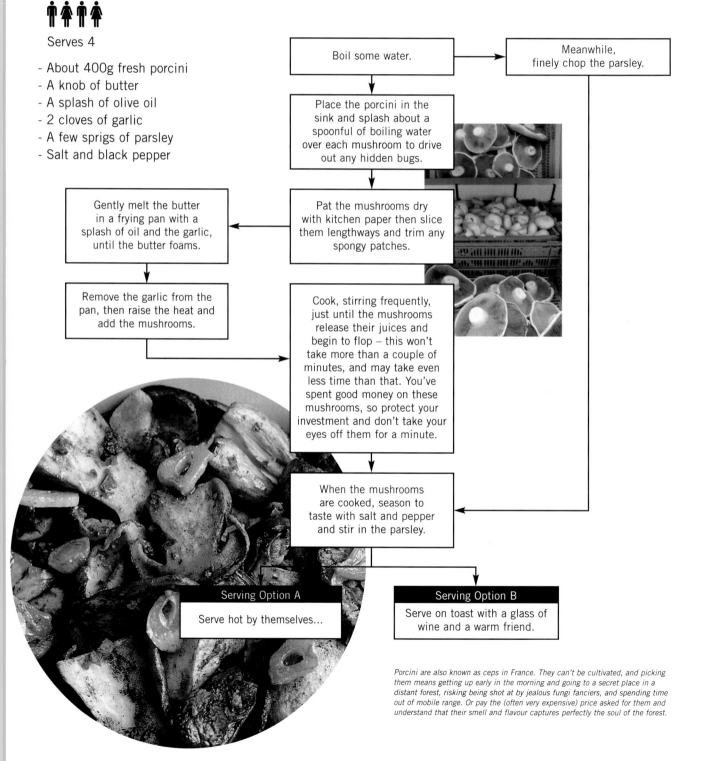

Porcini are also known as ceps in France. They can't be cultivated, and picking them means getting up early in the morning and going to a secret place in a distant forest, risking being shot at by jealous fungi fanciers, and spending time out of mobile range. Or pay the (often very expensive) price asked for them and understand that their smell and flavour captures perfectly the soul of the forest.

Velvet Spinach

Serves 4

- 80g spinach or a bag of ready-washed spinach
- A knob of butter
- 1 clove of garlic
- Grated Parmesan, or grated nutmeg, or nibbed walnuts
- 2 tablespoons of cream or crème fraîche (if you fancy)

Serve with grilled chicken (page 92), or anything else you think would taste great with this glossy spinach. Here's an idea: poach an egg. Make some toast. Put the spinach over the toast and the egg on top. That's kind of how Eggs Florentine came about.

Moses went to Mount Olive. So Popeye hit him.

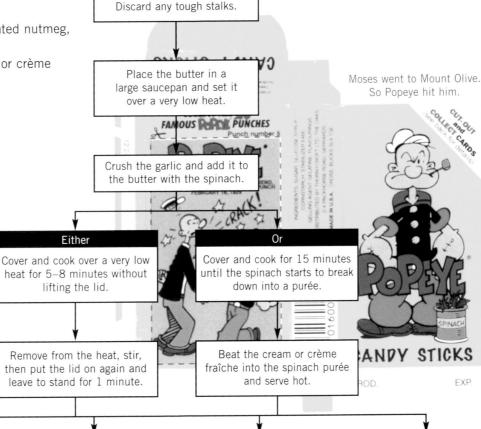

Rinse the spinach and shake off the excess water. Discard any tough stalks.

↓

Place the butter in a large saucepan and set it over a very low heat.

↓

Crush the garlic and add it to the butter with the spinach.

Either
Cover and cook over a very low heat for 5–8 minutes without lifting the lid.

Or
Cover and cook for 15 minutes until the spinach starts to break down into a purée.

Remove from the heat, stir, then put the lid on again and leave to stand for 1 minute.

Beat the cream or crème fraîche into the spinach purée and serve hot.

Serving Option A
Serve hot as it is.

Serving Option B
Grate a little fresh nutmeg over the spinach, stir briefly and serve.

Serving Option C
In a frying pan, toast a few nibbed walnuts until fragrant then serve them sprinkled over the hot spinach.

Serving Option D
Sprinkle a little grated Parmesan over the spinach and serve hot.

NẾP HƯƠNG N. GẠO N. NẾP NẾP BẮC THƠM

6.000 000 10.000

ITALIAN PASTA ℮ 500g
WAITROSE
Penne

ITALIAN PASTA ℮ 500g
WAITROSE
Penne

ITALIAN PASTA ℮ 500g
WAITROSE
Penne

price *commitment*

Waitrose
penne **45p**

ITALIAN
WAITROSE
Rigatoni
tubes

ITALIAN ℮ 500g
WAITROSE
Rigatoni
tubes

ITALIAN ℮ 500g
WAITROSE
Rigatoni
tubes

Persian Rice

Serves 4

- 600g/4 teacups of basmati rice
- A pinch of saffron threads
- 60g/4 tablespoons of lightly
  salted butter
- Salt

Inspir... ...*the subject of Persia...*

love and patience

G

rice above a...
to *darbori* a...

My gran...
town of Ka...
word 'Mar...
deduced that Manchester must be a very rich country and
that he would make his fortune there. Although it took him
nearly two years to walk to northern Europe, after a brief stop in
Paris, he eventually arrived in Southampton in 1914, where he
was given a new name, Jeff Joseph, and
a train ticket to Manchester.

From the moment he arrived, he
loved the place. Even the climate was a
blessed relief after the relentless dry
heat and scorpions of Kashan. Making
money by selling balls of string from a
barrow, and reinvesting his profits in
better stock, Jeff's business thrived as his
memory of Sarah's rice-making faded.

Marjorie's lesson was the same one
she gave me when I was 17 and hungry for a taste of my ancestors. Take at least one mug of rice for each guest. Because
domsiah, or for that matter any Iranian rice, hardly ever comes our
way, use the best, longest-grain basmati you can find. Muttering
imprecations to Zoroaster, spread the grains in a large bowl,
removing bits of husk and stones. Pour on boiling water and stir
like a mad mullah for a minute or so. Now, thinking pure
thoughts, rinse your rice in a colander with plenty of cold water
until it runs clear. Return your rice to a bowl and cover with
tepid salted water. Leave to soak: overnight is best, all day's not
bad, give it an hour at least.

When the time has come to cook it, meditate first on Jalada'bin
Rumi's advice that a mirror is a means of laughing in your own
face, then drain the rice and set a large lidded pan of salted water
to boil. When you have a rolling boil on the go, start adding the
rice spoon by spoon. The idea is that the constantly boiling water
stops the rice from sticking, so leave the pan uncovered, spoon
and stir, spoon and stir. Within 10 minutes, maybe less, choose a

My favourite treat is a bowl of

plain chillau rice, with lots of

butter, the yolk of an egg beaten in

and a spoon of thick yoghurt. And

a good gossip with Grandma

...en the grains are still slightly
...nsing with lukewarm water. Y...
...s elaborate performance is d...
...the rice, so take a bow and g...
...e pan, melt a tablespoon o...
...still-warm rice and stir carefu...
...e now you can take the op...
...tle flavourings. Some peop...
saffron which have been soaking in a thim...
Auntie Alma loves to add baby broad be...
For weddings, you might add sharp apric...
slivers of orange peel. And a New Year...
in March during the festival of Now Ro...
fresh fenugreek...

Anyway, yo...
pan, given it...
more butter...
yourself a *dam*...
of authenticity...
tea towel on y...
dish, remove...
top of the pan...
in the kitchen...
cloth. Jam th...

stretching it tight and securing the ends to...
the heat to high for one minute only, the...
rice over a very low flame for 25 minutes...
minutes, your rice will have turned into...
grain will be light and separate and de...
crispy golden crust known as *tardigeh* or *d*...
bottom of the pan should be carefully lifted...
ceremony to your guests, who should first...

As Sarah taught Grandma, who taugh...
about textures and harmony. This *chillau*...
with grilled or baked fish and meats, a...
slow-cooked stew, is the perfect count...
meld meats with fruits: lamb and apple, c...
or spinach and prune. My favourite treat...
chillau with lots of butter, the yolk of...
spoon of thick yoghurt. And a good gossi...

H

e — a

nte and then drain
ill have r
ed to tem
with Act
er for each guest,
his is an i
nity to i
a few st
of water,
d lots of
stachio kernels and
raditionally served
gon and chives.
got the rice in the
and dotted some
e top. Now find
f for the purposes
ve been wearing a
ead to make this
nce and cover the
t. Otherw
er for a cl
ver the a
op of the l
tinue stea
a further
od of angels: each
y flavour
has forme
d served
t dental i
Persian fo
marries beautifully
owl of *khoresh*, or
t. *Khoreshta* often
and pomegranate
is a bowl of plain
g beaten in a
Grandma.

PHOTOGRAPH BY DAVID LOFTUS

Boil some water.
Place the rice in a bowl and pour the boiling water over it, then drain through a strainer.

Rinse the rice under cold running water until the water runs clear.

Return the rice to the bowl, cover with lukewarm water and add a good pinch of salt. Leave to stand for at least 1 hour, and preferably overnight.

When ready to cook, bring a large pan of salted water to the boil.

Drain the soaked rice and add it to the boiling water a spoonful at a time, stirring the while, so the water is always boiling.

Simmer for about 8 minutes or until the grains are al dente, stirring continuously, whistling a selection from LingalongaMax.

Place the saffron threads in a cup and add 2 tablespoons of boiling water. Leave to infuse for 5–10 minutes. What a lovely colour.

Drain the rice thoroughly, and rinse with cold water in the colander.

Melt the butter in a large, heavy saucepan and add the drained rice, stirring with a wooden spoon and being careful not to break up the grains.

With the hand end of the wooden spoon, make 4 vent holes down to the bottom of the pan so that the rice will steam nicely.

Pour the saffron liquid over the rice.

Stretch a clean tea-towel over the top of the pan and jam on the lid. Fold the corners of the tea-towel back over the top of the lid.

Raise the heat under the pan to high for 1 minute, then turn it right down to the lowest possible flame. Leave to steam for 25 minutes.

Remove the pan from the heat. Fork through the rice and, if you like, add a bit more butter.

WARNING
Do not open the lid at any time!

Jam the cloth and lid back on top and leave the rice to stand for 10 minutes.

Serve, being sure to present the golden crust that has formed on the bottom of the pan to honoured guests.

Rice with Lentils and Caramelised Onions

👫/👫👫

Serves 2–4

- 400g canned brown lentils
- About 125g white basmati rice
- 1 onion
- Olive oil
- Salt
- A dollop of yoghurt

We're in the privileged position of being able to eat peasant food in non-peasant circumstances...

THE RICH MAN

'How I wish I could be really wealthy,' said Nasrudin to his cronies in the teahouse, 'like, say, Kara Mustafa the great lord, who has everything.'

'How strange that you should say that,' said the potter, 'because in my shop a few minutes ago Mustafa himself was saying how much he wished that he were a poor and simple man.'

'But that is only because he is rich already!' said Nasrudin; 'he has the wish and also knows the method of becoming poor. I only have the desire to be rich!'

Reprinted by permission from *Caravan of Dreams* by Idries Shah (Octagon Press Ltd, London).

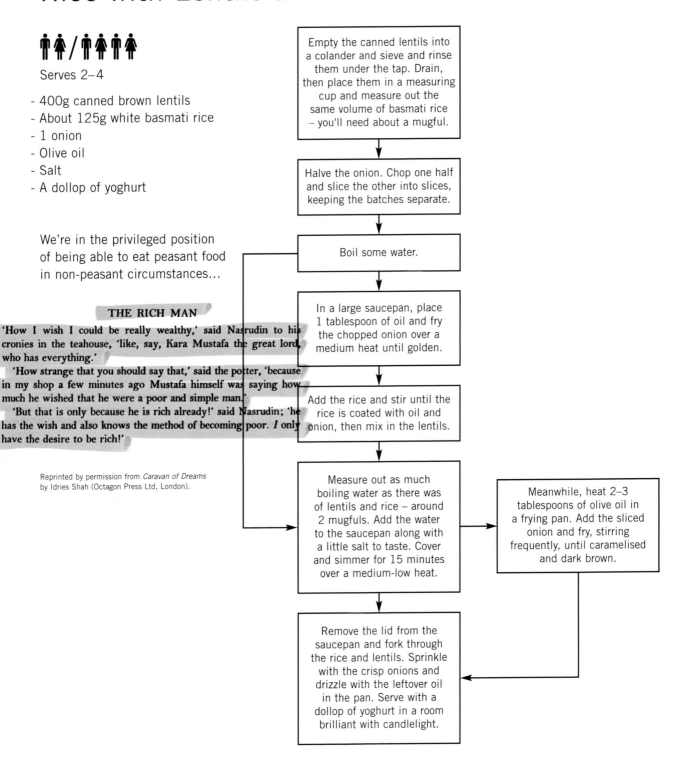

Empty the canned lentils into a colander and sieve and rinse them under the tap. Drain, then place them in a measuring cup and measure out the same volume of basmati rice – you'll need about a mugful.

↓

Halve the onion. Chop one half and slice the other into slices, keeping the batches separate.

↓

Boil some water.

↓

In a large saucepan, place 1 tablespoon of oil and fry the chopped onion over a medium heat until golden.

↓

Add the rice and stir until the rice is coated with oil and onion, then mix in the lentils.

↓

Measure out as much boiling water as there was of lentils and rice – around 2 mugfuls. Add the water to the saucepan along with a little salt to taste. Cover and simmer for 15 minutes over a medium-low heat.

→

Meanwhile, heat 2–3 tablespoons of olive oil in a frying pan. Add the sliced onion and fry, stirring frequently, until caramelised and dark brown.

↓

Remove the lid from the saucepan and fork through the rice and lentils. Sprinkle with the crisp onions and drizzle with the leftover oil in the pan. Serve with a dollop of yoghurt in a room brilliant with candlelight.

Saffron Risotto

Serves 4

- 30g/2 tablespoons of butter
- 900ml/3 mugs of vegetable or chicken stock (see pages 152–153)
- 400g/1½ mugs of risotto rice
- 1 glass of white wine
- 75g grated Parmesan cheese, plus extra to serve
- A pinch of saffron threads
- Salt and black pepper

WARNING

Don't leave this dish for a minute whilst it's cooking. Points will be deducted for going to the loo halfway through, taking non-urgent phone calls from gossipy acquaintances you don't really like, or answering the door to the Witnesses. You already know what they've got to tell you, anyway.

The perfect portion for this risotto is ten mouthfuls. More than that and the ambrosial meltiness of the dish becomes boring. Less than that and you'll be climbing the walls, wanting more. So, make too much, restrain yourself, then take a look at the leftover receipe on page 158.

Aim for a texture when the grains of rice still feel slightly resistant to the teeth, but have lost all their starchy stickiness. And really - don't leave your risotto for even a minute!

Melt the butter in a large, heavy saucepan over a low heat. In a separate pan, bring the stock to a simmer.

↓

Add the rice to the butter and cook, stirring with a wooden spoon, for about 2 minutes or until the rice is evenly coated.

↓

Raise the heat to medium and pour the wine into the rice. Allow it to bubble away until absorbed.

→ Meanwhile, grate the cheese. Place the saffron in a small cup and cover with 2 tablespoons of boiling water. Leave for up to 10 minutes whilst the saffron gives its soul to the water.

↓

Add a ladle of the hot stock to the rice and stir until all the liquid has been absorbed.

↓

Add another ladle of stock to the rice and stir until it has been absorbed. Continue in this fashion until the rice is al dente and the risotto is creamy and wavy.

↓

Stir in the saffron liquid, then the grated cheese. Taste it. Does it need salt or a grind of pepper?

Burghul Pilaf

Pearl Harbor Barley

Novarese Risotto

Serves 4, as it's lovely and rich

- 30g/2 tablespoons of butter
- 900ml/3 mugs of vegetable or chicken stock (see pages 152–153)
- 400g/1½ mugs of risotto rice
- 2–3 tablespoons of diced celery
- 1 glass of red wine
- 75g Parmesan cheese, plus extra to serve
- A small handful of parsley
- Salt and black pepper

POST CARD

THE ADDRESS TO BE WRITTEN ON THIS SIDE

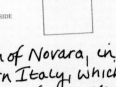

Inspired by the charming town of Novara, in the Piemonte part of northern Italy, which just happens to be near Vercelli (where the best risotto rice is grown), Alba (world centre for white truffles) and Barolo, where the big red wine comes from.

Melt the butter in a large, heavy saucepan over a low heat. In a separate pan, bring the stock to a simmer.

↓

Add the rice and celery to the butter and cook, stirring with a wooden spoon, for about 2 minutes or until the rice is evenly coated.

↓

Increase the heat to medium and pour the wine into the rice. Allow it to bubble away until absorbed. → Meanwhile, grate the cheese and chop the parsley.

↓

Add a ladleful of the hot stock to the rice and stir until all the liquid has been absorbed. As in the saffron risotto, don't leave this dish for a minute – not even to go to the loo. You should've gone before you started cooking.

↓

Add another ladle of stock to the rice and stir until it has been absorbed. Continue in this fashion until the rice is al dente and the risotto is creamy and wavy.

↓

The risotto is cooked when it will absorb hardly any more liquid. Stir in the grated cheese and the parsley and season to taste before serving.

NOVARA

Vercelli

 ALESSANDRA

Alba

Barolo

Burghul Pilaf

🚻🚻/🚻🚻🚹

Serves 4–6

- 500g medium or coarse burghul
- 900ml salted water,
  or vegetable stock,
  or chicken stock,
  or meat stock (see pages 152–153)
- 2 tablespoons of butter
- 200g halloumi,
  or 125g pine nuts,
  or 2–3 tablespoons tomato paste,
  or Roasted Sweet and Hot Pepper
  Mush (see page 16)
- Salt

In many parts of the Middle East, burghul is the grain you're most likely to be offered to eat. Grocery stores carry it in lots of grinds, from very fine to coarse, though the stuff sold in Europe is nearly all medium. A Turkish or Lebanese cook would use the fine stuff to roll around minced meat, fish or potato rissoles called kibbeh (that's the problem with so many chefs, of course, they're a bunch of rissoles). Coarse burghul most often goes into tabbouleh, which, unlike Western versions, contains predominately green herbs and scallions, with just a bit of chopped tomato on top... Here's how to cook it to eat like a rice or pasta dish.

Place the burghul in a sieve and rinse under cold water until the water runs clear.

↓

Bring the stock, or water, to the boil in a large saucepan.

↓

Add the burghul, stir once, cover and turn the heat right down to the lowest possible setting.

↓

Cook for 10–15 minutes.

↓

Remove from the heat and fork through the burghul. Cover and leave to stand for 10 minutes, during which time the burghul will continue to expand.

↓

Just before serving, stir the butter through the pilaf so that it melts.

Serving Option A
Dice the halloumi and stir it through the pilaf.

Serving Option C
Toast the pine nuts in a frying pan, stirring constantly, until golden, then stir them through the pilaf.

Serving Option E
Stir the tomato paste or pepper purée through the pilaf until the grains are red.

Serving Option B
Eat disturbing amounts straight out of the pan.

Serving Option D
Serve with Roasted Chicken (page 93), Grilled Meat (page 114) or Meatballs with Flatbread and Yoghurt Sauce (page 116).

Pearl Harbor Barley

PEARL BAILEY
Hello Pearlie Mae

👤👤👤👤/👤👤👤👤👤👤

Serves 4–6

- About 1.2 litres of beef, lamb or rich vegetable stock (see page 152)
- 500g pearl barley
- 1 radicchio
- Salt and black pepper

Pearling a grain involves putting it through a roller mill in Scotland where the spiked rollers remove the tough outer husk. Unhulled, or pot barley takes ages to cook. It may be worthy, and heartily enjoyed by men in beards and women in dirndl skirts, but so is brown rice, saving the whale and free love. Come to think of it...

Bring the stock to the boil in a large pot.

↓

Add the barley and boil hard for 5 minutes.

↓

Turn the heat right down, cover the pot and leave the barley to cook for 30 minutes. → Meanwhile, shred the radicchio into ribbons with a knife or pair of scissors.

↓

After 30 minutes, check the barley to make sure it is not scorching on the bottom of the pan and fork through.

↓

Continue cooking until tender, perhaps another 5–10 minutes, adding more liquid if necessary or leaving the pot uncovered so that any excess liquid can evaporate.

↓

Remove from the heat, stir through the radicchio. Taste it. Does it taste good? Does it need more salt and/or pepper?

↓

Cover and leave to stand for another 5 minutes before serving.

↓

Listen to old recordings by Pearl Bailey.

Pearl Bailey, *Hello Pearlie Mae*
©1983 MCA Records Inc.

Serving Option A
This is very nice with Pumpkin Stew (page 40).

Serving Option B
It's also delicious with Chicken with Sweet Peppers (page 106).

Serving Option C
Served with Lancashire Hot Pot (page 115) it's a taste of home, if you're from Up North.

Spaghetti with Butter and Shaved Truffles, or perhaps Truffle Oil, or even Truffle Paste

Spaghetti with Butter and Shaved Truffles, or perhaps Truffle Oil, or even Truffle Paste

'Please me, pleease me, pleeease me ba-by, 'til I lose contro-ohol....'

Serves 4

- 500g spaghetti
- 50g Parmesan cheese
- 100g butter
- Salt and black pepper

OPTION A
- A small fresh truffle the size of a large marble or a squash ball if you can afford it. Don't go for the truffles preserved in liquid – they've lost their cobblers by the time you get them home

OPTION B
- 1 teaspoon of truffle oil

OPTION C
- 1 tablespoon of truffle paste

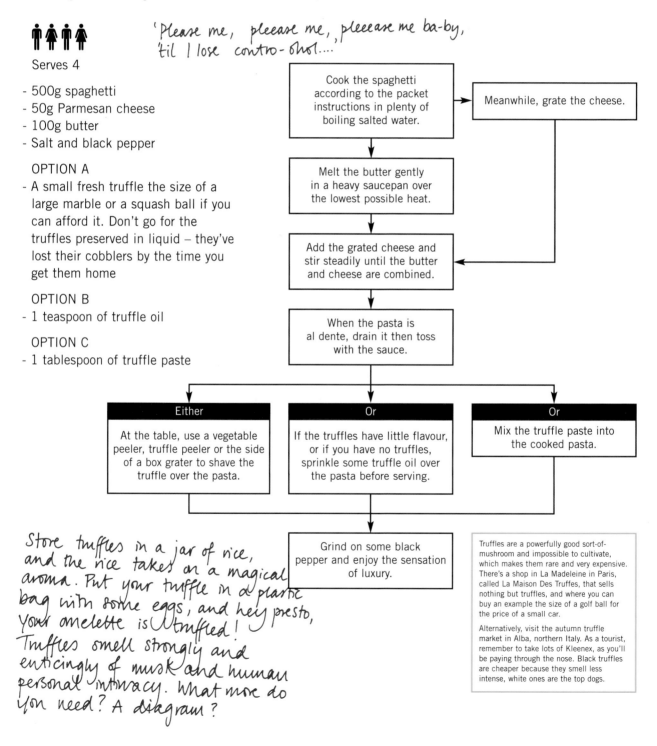

Cook the spaghetti according to the packet instructions in plenty of boiling salted water.

Meanwhile, grate the cheese.

Melt the butter gently in a heavy saucepan over the lowest possible heat.

Add the grated cheese and stir steadily until the butter and cheese are combined.

When the pasta is al dente, drain it then toss with the sauce.

Either
At the table, use a vegetable peeler, truffle peeler or the side of a box grater to shave the truffle over the pasta.

Or
If the truffles have little flavour, or if you have no truffles, sprinkle some truffle oil over the pasta before serving.

Or
Mix the truffle paste into the cooked pasta.

Grind on some black pepper and enjoy the sensation of luxury.

Store truffles in a jar of rice, and the rice takes on a magical aroma. Put your truffle in a plastic bag with some eggs, and hey presto, your omelette is truffled! Truffles smell strongly and enticingly of musk and human personal intimacy. What more do you need? A diagram?

Truffles are a powerfully good sort-of-mushroom and impossible to cultivate, which makes them rare and very expensive. There's a shop in La Madeleine in Paris, called La Maison Des Truffes, that sells nothing but truffles, and where you can buy an example the size of a golf ball for the price of a small car.

Alternatively, visit the autumn truffle market in Alba, northern Italy. As a tourist, remember to take lots of Kleenex, as you'll be paying through the nose. Black truffles are cheaper because they smell less intense, white ones are the top dogs.

Fresh or Dried Linguine with Pesto, Green Beans and Potato

Serves 6 because it's so delicious

- 250g waxy potatoes
- 200g French green beans, ideally the very thin ones
- 500g fresh or dried linguine
- 4 tablespoons of pine nuts
- Parmesan cheese – as much as you fancy
- 150g fresh basil pesto
- Salt and black pepper

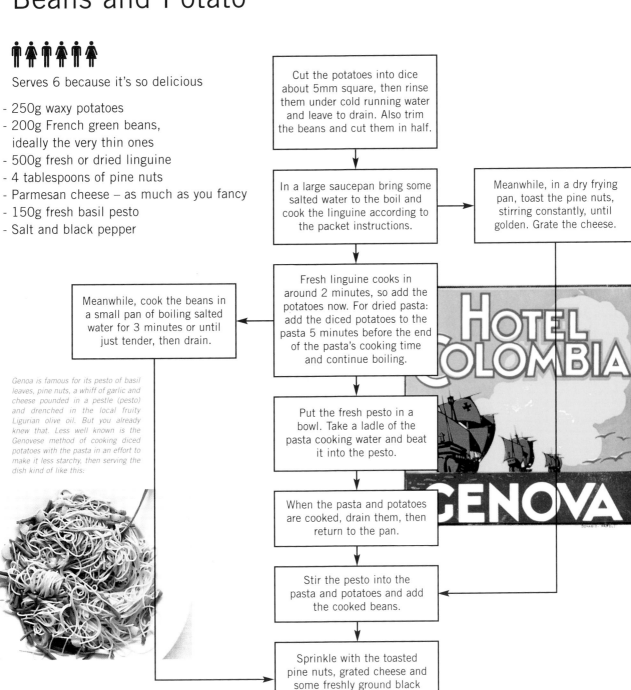

Cut the potatoes into dice about 5mm square, then rinse them under cold running water and leave to drain. Also trim the beans and cut them in half.

In a large saucepan bring some salted water to the boil and cook the linguine according to the packet instructions.

Meanwhile, in a dry frying pan, toast the pine nuts, stirring constantly, until golden. Grate the cheese.

Fresh linguine cooks in around 2 minutes, so add the potatoes now. For dried pasta: add the diced potatoes to the pasta 5 minutes before the end of the pasta's cooking time and continue boiling.

Meanwhile, cook the beans in a small pan of boiling salted water for 3 minutes or until just tender, then drain.

Put the fresh pesto in a bowl. Take a ladle of the pasta cooking water and beat it into the pesto.

When the pasta and potatoes are cooked, drain them, then return to the pan.

Stir the pesto into the pasta and potatoes and add the cooked beans.

Sprinkle with the toasted pine nuts, grated cheese and some freshly ground black pepper before serving.

Genoa is famous for its pesto of basil leaves, pine nuts, a whiff of garlic and cheese pounded in a pestle (pesto) and drenched in the local fruity Ligurian olive oil. But you already knew that. Less well known is the Genovese method of cooking diced potatoes with the pasta in an effort to make it less starchy, then serving the dish kind of like this:

Tagliatelle with Bottarga and Red Chile

Serves 4

- 500g tagliatelle
- 1 small red chile
- A handful of parsley leaves, if you like
- 2 tablespoons of olive oil, plus extra to serve
- About 60g bottarga
- Salt and black pepper

In a large pan of boiling salted water, cook the pasta according to the packet instructions.

Meanwhile, slice the chile down the middle, and remove the seeds (unless you're a thrill-seeking pervert with no sense of delicacy). Shred the parsley and set it aside.

In a small frying pan, heat the olive oil and fry the chile for 2–3 minutes.

When the pasta is cooked, drain thoroughly then toss it with the chile and parsley, if you like parsley, adding extra olive oil if desired.

Grate the bottarga over the top of the pasta and serve immediately, with freshly ground black pepper, for that Sicilian touch.

You may have seen this described in Italian as tagliatelle con bottarga. Bottarga (boutargue in French and Arabic) is pressed, dried fish roes, usually from tunny or mullet, which is grated or sliced thinly over dishes like this. Bottarga's fearfully expensive, but lasts for ages, and is sometimes available from Greek and Italian shops. This version uses the stuff you can get in tins or from the fresh fish counter - try not to use the smoked roes, as they'll overpower all the other flavours.

Penne with Marcella Hazan's Favourite Tomato Sauce

Serves 4

- 2 x 400g cans plum tomatoes
- About 80g butter
- ½ onion
- 500g penne, spaghetti or any other pasta you've got sitting around
- A chunk of Parmesan cheese for grating
- Salt and black pepper

Put the canned tomatoes in a heavy saucepan with the butter and a pinch of salt if desired and place over a medium heat.

↓

Peel the skin from the onion half and add it to the saucepan.

↓

Cook, stirring constantly with a wooden spoon, until the mixture starts to bubble.

↓

Turn the heat down to low and, when the butter has melted, use the back of the spoon to squeeze the tomatoes against the side of the saucepan until you have a smooth sauce.

↓

Cook for up to 45 minutes, until the sauce is very smooth and has a buttery sheen. →

Meanwhile, cook the pasta in a large pan of boiling salted water according to the packet instructions.

↓

Just before serving, remove the onion from the sauce – it can be rinsed off and used in soup or stock making (see pages 152–153).

↓

Taste the sauce. Does it need salt? Then toss with the drained cooked pasta. Serve with freshly grated Parmesan cheese.

*Anybody really serious about Italian food should read Marcella Hazan's books. Nobody researches or explains the subject as comprehensively, and for only thousands of dollars a week you can join her on the cookery courses she runs at her Venetian palazzo.

134 LEE'S

SEA FOODS

134

ASHLEY
Sub-Aqua Guide
Fish of the British Isles

LABRUS BERGYLTA
Ballan Wrasse 40cm

♂

♀

ZEUS FABER
John Dory 40cm

CRENILABRUS MELOPS
Corkwing Wrasse 20cm

LABRUS MIXTUS
Cuckoo Wrasse 35cm

BLENNIUS OCELLARIS
Butterfly Blenny 20cm

RAJA CLAVATA
Thornback Ray 85cm

TORPEDO MARMORATA
Marbled Electric Ray 60cm

MERLANGIUS MERLANGUS
Whiting 60cm

PARABLENNIUS GATTORUGINE
Tompot Blenny 30cm

TRISOPTERUS LUSCUS
Bib 30

Cod 120cm

MULLUS SURMULETUS
Red Mullet 40cm

CHELON LABROSUS
Thick Lipped Grey Mullet 75cm

DENTEX LABRAX
Bass 100cm

POLLACHIUS POLLACHIUS
Pollack 100cm

MELANOGRAMMUS AEGLEFINUS
Haddock 75cm

SCOMBER SCOMBRUS
Atlantic Mackerel 50cm

POLLACHIUS VIRENS
Saith, Pollock or Coley 100cm

TRISOPTERUS MINUTUS
Poor Cod 20cm

TAURULUS BUBALIS
Long Spined Sea Scorpion 17cm

LOPHIUS PISCATORIUS
Angler Fish 150cm

HIPPOCAMPUS RAMULOSUS
Sea Horse 15cm

SCOPHTHALMUS RHOMBUS
Brill 70cm

PLEURONECTES PLATESSA
Plaice 60cm

PSETTA MAXIMA
Turbot 80cm

LIMANDA LIMANDA
Dab 25cm

MICROSTOMUS KITT
Lemon Sole 40cm

SOLEA SOLEA
Dover Sole 40cm

For personal safety & protection of all marine life, do not touch or molest.
Ashley Sub-Aqua Guides. Kuan Yin, Gladjoli St., Madliena, NXR09 Malta. G.C. All rights reserved. © 1996

'Fish should taste like smell like fish, it's too Delmonicos, New York,

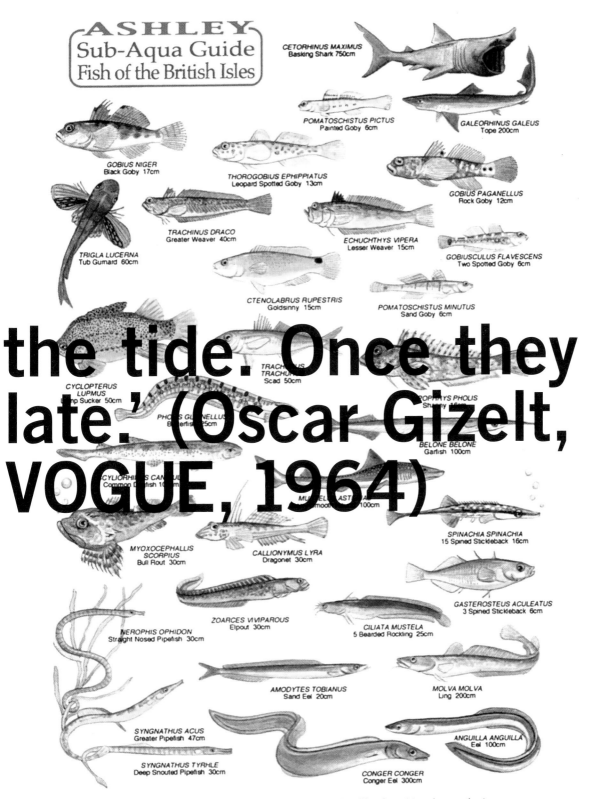

the tide. Once they late.' (Oscar Gizelt, VOGUE, 1964)

Chargrilled Fish

Serves 2

- 2 portions of fish, whole fish (gutted), fillets or steaks
- 2 tablespoons of olive oil
- Salt and black pepper

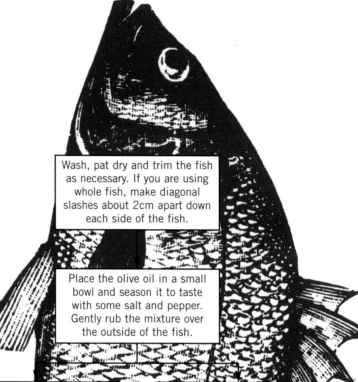

Wash, pat dry and trim the fish as necessary. If you are using whole fish, make diagonal slashes about 2cm apart down each side of the fish.

Place the olive oil in a small bowl and season it to taste with some salt and pepper. Gently rub the mixture over the outside of the fish.

Either	Or
Heat the chargrill over the highest setting until it is very hot.	Heat an overhead grill until very hot.
When the chargrill is hot, reduce the heat to medium and place the fish on the pan. Cook it for 3 minutes on each side – an older or meatier fish such as tuna will require a minute or two longer.	When the overhead grill is hot, place the fish underneath it about a handspan away from the heat source. Cook for about 3 minutes on each side.

WARNING

Be aware that this type of kitchen work can make a place smoky. Turn the extractor hood on or open a window. It's tricky trying to impress someone with your artistry and hospitality if the smoke alarm's going off.

Grilled fish should be served with a smile and a finger bowl. A finger bowl should be big enough to put all the fingers in at once, and should be half-filled with warm water and something aromatic, such as a slice of lime, lemon or orange. Extra napkins with finger bowls are also a good idea, as is a splash of orange blossom water.

Charred Prawns over Walnut Tarator

Serves 4

For the prawns:
- 900g–1kg fresh or frozen large raw prawns in shells (this is 3–4 king prawns each)
- 6 tablespoons of olive oil
- ½ teaspoon of salt
- Black pepper
- 2 cloves of garlic or 2 teaspoons of chopped shallot or young onion
- 1 small red chile

For the walnut tarator:
- 4 slices of stale white bread
- 3–4 tablespoons of milk
- 100g walnuts
- 2 large cloves of garlic
- 180ml olive oil
- Salt and black pepper

For the Prawns

Place the prawns in a large Tupperware container with the olive oil, salt and several twists of ground black pepper.

Chop the garlic, shallot or onion and add it to the prawns.
Seed the chile, chop it very very finely and add it to the prawns.

Leave to marinate for 1 to 2 hours, out of the fridge. If the prawns are frozen, they will defrost during this time.

Turn up those arabesque beats and imagine yourself at Bebek, up the Bosphorous from Istanbul old town, under the huge suspension bridge to Asia, where the gypsy food stalls perfume the warm air with the eat-me-now! smell of prawns grilling over charcoal.

For the Walnut Tarator

Meanwhile, make the tarator. Lay out the bread on a tray and sprinkle it with the milk to bring it back to life.

Finely chop the walnuts and garlic together.

Either

Transfer to a mortar, add the bread and start pounding with the pestle to combine and break down the mixture. Slowly work in the olive oil until you have a granular paste.

Or

Add the bread on to the board and keep chopping and mixing with the heel of the knife, slowly adding the olive oil to create a granular paste.

When ready to cook the prawns, heat a ridged griddle over a high heat for several minutes until searingly hot. Add the prawns and immediately turn the heat down to medium. Cook for 1½ minutes on each side until the prawn shells are an appetising burnished-copper colour.

This is a good time to havesome orange blossom water (see page 38) around the place for washing fishy fingers with.

Season the tarator with salt and pepper, according to taste.

Suck the shells then peel the prawns and dip them in the tarator, pretending you're on Simi and are not really looking at the nudists.

Serve the prawns on a plate with the walnut tarator piled in the middle. Provide two finger bowls, one for cleaning your fingers and the other for discarding the shells.

Sardines Stuffed with Onion, Parsley and Lemon

Serves 2 with tattoos or 2 without

- 4–6 medium sardines
- 1 large onion
- 1 tablespoon of olive oil
- A large handful of curly parsley
- ¼ lemon
- Maldon Sea salt
- Crusty baguette

Only use fresh sardines for this. Tinned ones are all very well, and sometimes come in tins that are minor design classics; however, they're already cooked and have lost that zingy freshness that we're looking for here.

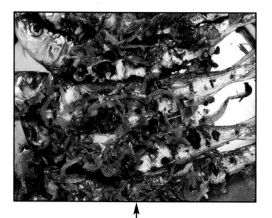

Get your fishmonger to gut and clean the sardines for you. At home, rinse them inside and out and pat dry with kitchen paper.

↓

Chop the onion as finely as possible and place it in a small saucepan with a tablespoon of olive oil. Cook over a low heat for 10–15 minutes, stirring constantly, until the onion is very soft but not brown.

↓

When the onion is soft, raise the heat a little and add a tablespoon of hot water. Cook until the water has been absorbed, then add another tablespoon of hot water. Keep doing this for 10–15 minutes or until you have about a teacup of sweet onion pulp.

↓

Transfer the onion pulp to a bowl. Chop the parsley and add it to the onion, then grate the rind from the lemon quarter and stir it into the mixture.

↓

Heat the grill. Stuff the mixture into the cleaned sardines and use a sharp knife to slash the fish diagonally down to the bone 3 or 4 times on each side.

↓

Rub the outsides of the fish with olive oil and salt then, when the grill is very hot, cook the sardines for 3 minutes on each side. This can also be done on a barbeque.

↓

Serve hot, right now, inside your crunchy baguette.

Tattoos ©1999 Johnson & Mayer Inc.

White Fish Chermoula

👤👤👤👤👤👤

Serves 6 polite people

- 1kg white fish fillets, such as cod, coley or whiting
- 2 large handfuls of flat parsley
- 2 large handfuls of coriander
- 4 or 5 cloves of garlic
- 1 lemon
- 1 small hot chile
- 1 teaspoon of cumin
- 1 teaspoon of cayenne pepper
- Salt
- About 500ml extra virgin olive oil

This dish is as easy as pulling a stranger on a Friday night in Camden, but it is much more impressive.

Wash and dry the fish, trimming it of any skin or stray bones, and cut it into bite-sized pieces.

Chop all the herbs. Peel and smash the garlic. Juice the lemon. Slice open the chile lengthways and remove the seeds, unless you're a masochist, in which case rub your fingers in your eyes as well. Finely chop the chile.

Place the fish, herbs, garlic, chile and lemon juice in a large pot with the cumin, cayenne and 2 teaspoons of salt. Drench the lot in olive oil until it is more or less covered, put a lid on the pot and leave it in the fridge for an hour, or longer.

When ready to cook, put the pot, uncovered, over a low heat and cook for 30–45 minutes, stirring occasionally. Before serving, taste it and add more salt if necessary.

Serving Option A	Serving Option B	Serving Option C	Serving Option D
Serve with Persian Rice (see page 52).	Serve with couscous.	Serve with Burghul Pilaf (see page 60).	Serve with a pair of bongos or a single bong to accompany the Rai music with undulating hips and ululating lips.

Prawns and Wilted Rocket

Serves 2 close friends,
with any luck

- 400g tiny prawns
- 2 lemons
- 1 small fresh hot chile, chopped
- Salt
- A splash of olive oil
- 1 clove of garlic
- 2 handfuls of wild rocket

Place the prawns in a bowl. Juice the lemons, chop the chile and add them to the prawns with a little salt. Leave to marinate somewhere cold for a couple of hours.

↓

When ready to cook, drain the prawns and reserve the lemon juice.

↓

Heat the oil in a large pan. Smash the garlic and gently fry it just until it colours, then remove the garlic from the oil.

↓

Throw in the drained prawns and cook them fast over a high heat, then pour in a little of the lemon juice and boil it fast to reduce it. This part should take less than 2 minutes.

↓

Break up the rocket with your hands and, almost at the moment it hits the pan, stir quickly then tip the lot into a salad bowl.

↓

That's it.

Try this one out on a friend

ABSENCE

Every night I scan
the heavens with my eyes
seeking the star
that you are contemplating.

I question travellers
from the four corners of the earth
hoping to meet one
who has breathed your fragrance.

When the wind blows
I make sure it blows in my face:
the breeze might bring me
news of you.

I wander over roads
without aim, without purpose.
Perhaps a song
will sound your name.

Secretly I study
every face I see
hoping against hope
to glimpse a trace of your beauty.

Abū Bakr al-Ṭurṭūshī
(1059–1126) (Eastern Andalusia)

Poems of Eastern Andalucia, Franzen, City Lights 1989

Mackerel with Sharp Fruit

Marinated Scallops on the Half-Shell

Charred Prawns over Walnut Tarator

KEVIN GOULD

Marinated Scallops on the Half-Shell

👤👩👤👩/👤👩

4 as a starter/2 as a main

- 12 fresh scallops on the shell
- 1 orange
- Olive oil
- 1 clove of garlic
- Dried nori flakes (if your supermarket has them in the ethnic or sushi section) or chopped flat-leaf parsley
- Salt

fig.1. The scallop shells make lousy ashtrays afterwards, but don't let that stop you...

If they're clammed shut, ask your fishmonger to open them for you, making sure you keep the frilly skirts from inside for stock. Alternatively, buy them already on the half-shell.

Clean the scallops, corals and shells and pat dry with kitchen paper.

Set aside 6 of the best-looking shells to serve the scallops.

Place the scallops in a bowl. Juice the orange and add it to the scallops with 2 tablespoons of olive oil. Smash the garlic clove and add it to the bowl with a little salt.

Stir to coat then cover and marinate in the fridge for about 2 hours.

Just before you are ready to serve, heat a griddle or heavy frying pan for several minutes or until very hot. Grease it with a smidgen of the oil.

Add the scallops and corals to the griddle and immediately turn the heat down to medium. Cook for 30 seconds on each side.

Serve two scallops and their corals per person, arranged on the reserved scallop shells and sprinkled with some nori flakes or chopped parsley.

Serving Option A

Serve over crushed ice.

Serving Option C

Serve over fresh seaweed.

Serving Option B

Serve only 1 person, and eat twice as much.

Mackerel with Sharp Fruit

Serves 2 people who like mackerel with sharp fruit

- 2 mackerel (gutted)
- A small handful of flat-leaf parsley
- 2 tablespoons of olive oil
- 1 tablespoon of butter

For the sauce:
- 225g ready-to-eat dried apricots
- 2 lemons

Tommy Cooper:
I went scuba diving, to catch some fish.
There I was, wet suit, face mask, oxygen cylinders on the sea bed.
I saw this bloke coming towards me, moustache, sports jacket, grey flannel trousers.
'What are you doing?' I asked.
'I'm drowning.'

Boil some water. Place the dried apricots in a bowl and cover them with the boiling water. Leave to stand for 45 minutes until the apricots are plump and juicy.

↓

Drain the apricots, reserving the soaking water. Chop the apricots as small as possible.

↓

Transfer the apricots and the soaking water to a saucepan and place over a moderate heat. Bring to the boil and cook for about 45 minutes, adding more water as necessary and using a wooden spoon to help break the apricots down to a purée.

→ Meanwhile, wash the mackerel and pat dry. Use a sharp knife to score the sides of the fish at 2cm intervals.

↓

Place a few parsley stalks inside each fish, making sure you reserve some to use as a garnish.

↓

Juice the lemons and add to the apricot sauce a little at a time until you have a pleasingly sharp-sweet sauce. Keep the sauce warm.

↓

Heat the olive oil and butter in a large frying pan and add the fish. Cook for 2½–3 minutes on each side so that the mackerel are crisp on the outside and soft inside.

↓

Make a pool of apricot sauce on each serving plate and top with the fried mackerel. Snip some of the reserved parsley stalks over the top of the plate to make it look pretty and professional. The oiliness of the fish will compliment the sharp apricot sauce very nicely.

Built-in kitchens include all sorts of appliances – why not sound systems? Good cooking and good music go together perfectly. So switch on your favourite tunes, get lost in the beats and create some damn fine foods!

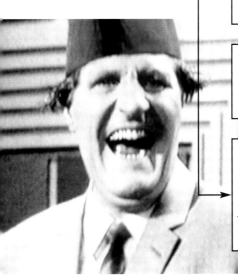

A Feztival of Fun with Tommy Cooper
©1999 Granada Media Group Ltd.

Elban Mussels over Stale Bread

Serves 2

- 350g/1 pint/600ml mussels
- 375ml white wine (half a bottle)
- 125ml olive oil
- 1 red chile
- 4–5 cloves of garlic
- A few sprigs of oregano
- 2 slices of stale bread, preferably focaccia, ciabatta or baguette
- Salt and black pepper

Scrub the mussels and remove any beards. Discard any that are broken or that do not close when tapped sharply.

Place the mussels in a large saucepan and add the wine and olive oil.

Slice the chile lengthways, scoop out the seeds and add it to the pan along with the peeled garlic and the leaves from the oregano.

Cover and bring the mussels to the boil, then turn the heat right down and cook gently for 10 minutes without removing the lid.

Place the stale bread in the bottom of 2 high-sided bowls.

Uncover the pan and lift the mussels out using a slotted spoon, transferring them to the serving bowls.

Raise the heat if necessary and allow the broth to boil hard for 2–3 minutes to make a slightly sticky but still runny sauce.

Taste the sauce.
Does it taste lovely? Does it need more salt and/or pepper?
Pour the liquid over the mussels and serve.

WARNING
Don't be tempted to eat any mussels that remain clamped shut after cooking. This is nature's way to avoid getting Elban Belly.

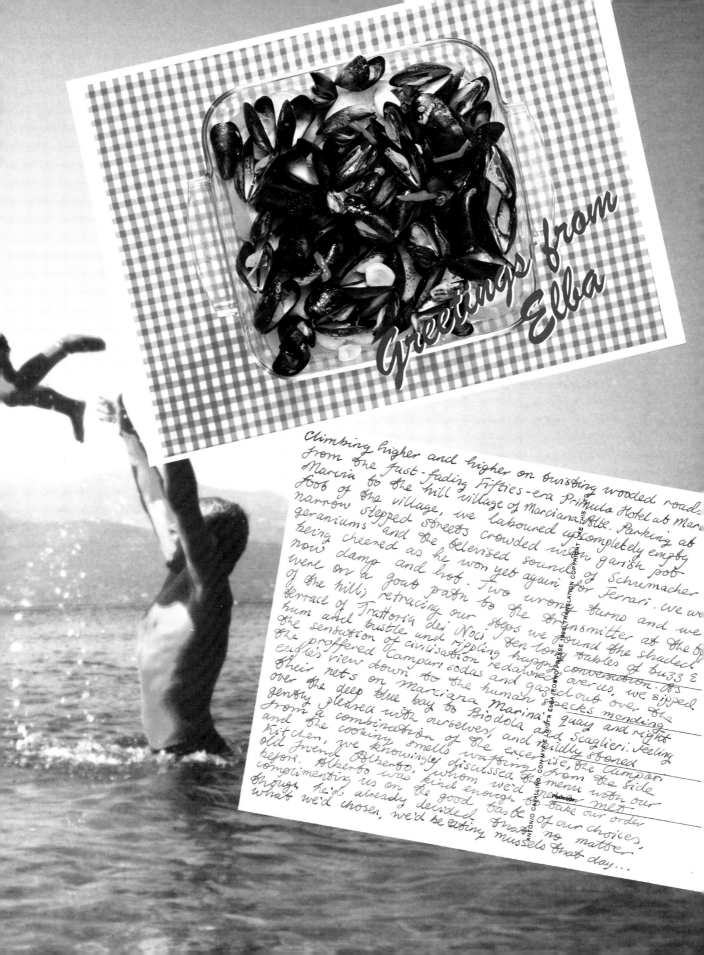

Greetings from Elba

Climbing higher and higher on twisting wooded roads from the fast-fading Fifties-era Primula Hotel at Mar. Marina to the hill village of Marciana Alta. Parking at foot of the village, we laboured up completely empty narrow stepped streets crowded with garish pot geraniums and the televised sound of Schumacher being cheered as he won yet again for Ferrari. We we now damp and hot. Two wrong turns and we went on a goat path to the transmitter at the t of the hill; retracing our steps we found the shaded terrace of Trattoria dei Noci. Den long tables of buzz & hum and bustle and rippling happy conversation. As the sensation of civilisation redawned over us, we sipped the proffered Campari sodas and gazed out over the eagle's view down to the human specks mending their nets on Marciana Marina quay and right over the deep blue bay to Biodola and Scaglieri. Feeling gently pleased with ourselves, and mildly stoned from a combination of the exercise, the Campari and the cooking smells wafting from the side kitchen, we knowingly discussed the menu with our old friend Alberto, whom we'd never met before. Alberto was kind enough to take our order complimenting us on the good taste of our choices, though he'd already decided that no matter what we'd chosen, we'd be eating mussels that day...

Postcode

Panfried Monkfish with Roast Garlic

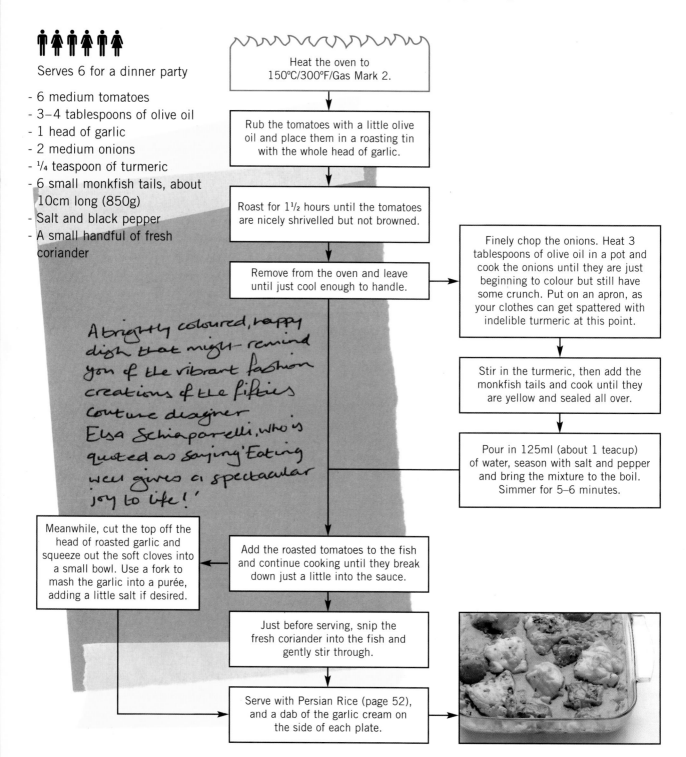

Serves 6 for a dinner party

- 6 medium tomatoes
- 3–4 tablespoons of olive oil
- 1 head of garlic
- 2 medium onions
- ¼ teaspoon of turmeric
- 6 small monkfish tails, about 10cm long (850g)
- Salt and black pepper
- A small handful of fresh coriander

Heat the oven to 150°C/300°F/Gas Mark 2.

Rub the tomatoes with a little olive oil and place them in a roasting tin with the whole head of garlic.

Roast for 1½ hours until the tomatoes are nicely shrivelled but not browned.

Remove from the oven and leave until just cool enough to handle.

Finely chop the onions. Heat 3 tablespoons of olive oil in a pot and cook the onions until they are just beginning to colour but still have some crunch. Put on an apron, as your clothes can get spattered with indelible turmeric at this point.

Stir in the turmeric, then add the monkfish tails and cook until they are yellow and sealed all over.

Pour in 125ml (about 1 teacup) of water, season with salt and pepper and bring the mixture to the boil. Simmer for 5–6 minutes.

A brightly coloured, happy dish that might remind you of the vibrant fashion creations of the fifties couture designer Elsa Schiaparelli, who is quoted as saying 'Eating well gives a spectacular joy to life!'

Meanwhile, cut the top off the head of roasted garlic and squeeze out the soft cloves into a small bowl. Use a fork to mash the garlic into a purée, adding a little salt if desired.

Add the roasted tomatoes to the fish and continue cooking until they break down just a little into the sauce.

Just before serving, snip the fresh coriander into the fish and gently stir through.

Serve with Persian Rice (page 52), and a dab of the garlic cream on the side of each plate.

Poached Salmon with Walnut and Celery

Serves 4

- A handful of coriander seeds
- A handful of white peppercorns
- 4 salmon fillets
- Salt
- 200–300ml white wine
  such as Muscadet

For the sauce:
- 50g walnuts
- 1 small celery stalk
- A small handful of dill
- 250–300g fromage frais
- Salt and black pepper

In a small frying pan, dry toast the coriander seeds until fragrant. Remove from the heat and crack them and the peppercorns open using a rolling pin or pestle and mortar.

Place the salmon fillets in a large deep-lidded frying pan and add the coriander, peppercorns and some salt. Cover the fish using a mixture of half wine and half water.

Place the pan over a moderate heat and bring the liquid to the boil. Cover with the lid, then remove the pan from the heat and leave it to stand for 10 minutes.

Meanwhile, make the sauce. In the small frying pan, dry toast the walnuts until fragrant, then remove from the heat and chop.

Use a vegetable peeler to destring the celery, then finely dice it.

Finely chop the dill then stir it into the fromage frais along with the walnuts and celery. Season the sauce to taste with salt and black pepper.

When the fish is cooked, skim the liquid if necessary then carefully remove the fillets from the liquid. Let them dry briefly before serving with the sauce.

Empty meadows, white wine chilling in the shallows of slow-moving rivers, the heady smell of fresh grass, crumpled linen trousers, dragonflies, hot lips, see-through motives…

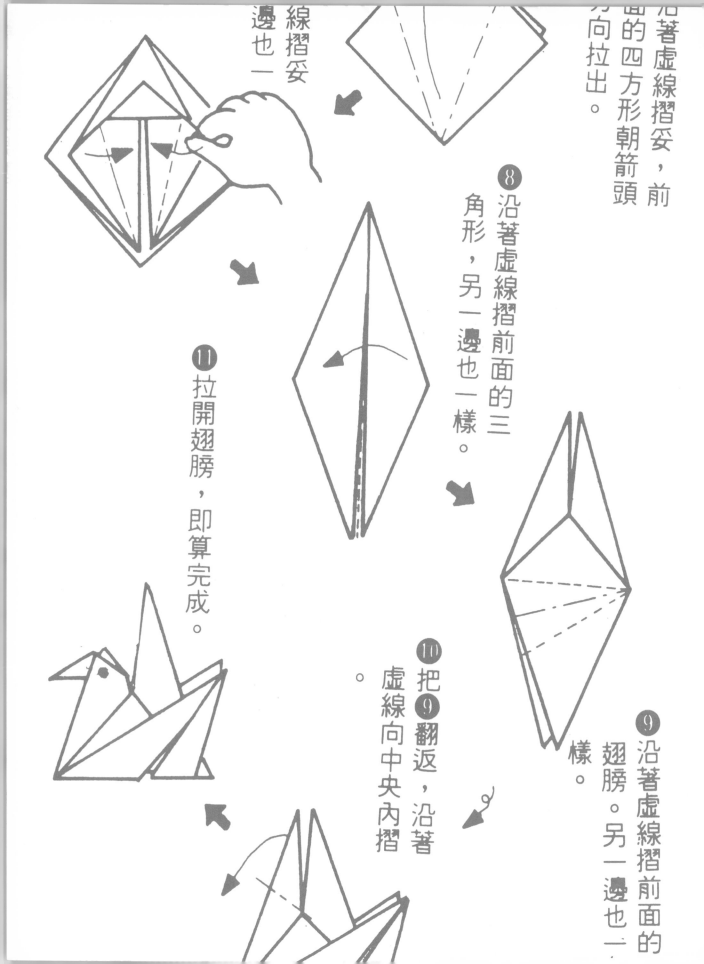

沿著虛線摺妥，前面的四方形朝箭頭方向拉出。

⑧沿著虛線摺前面的三角形，另一邊也一樣。

線摺妥邊也一

⑪拉開翅膀，即算完成。

⑨沿著虛線摺前面的翅膀。另一邊也一樣。

⑩把⑨翻返，沿著虛線向中央內摺。

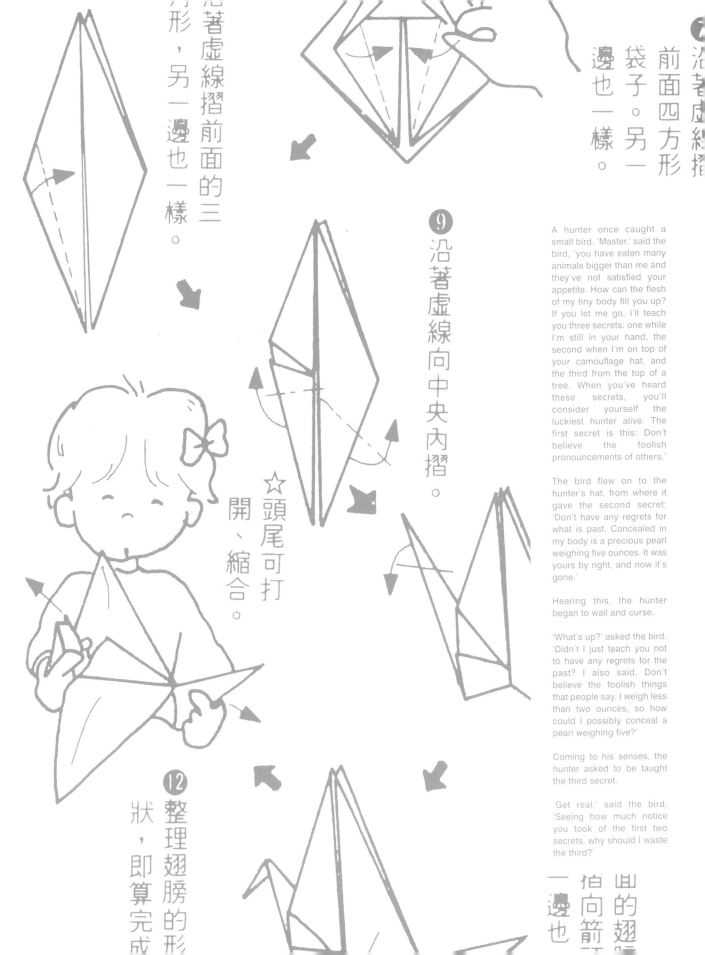

沿著虛線摺
前面四方形
袋子。另一
邊也一樣。

沿著虛線摺前面的三
角形，另一邊也一樣。

⑨ 沿著虛線向中央內摺。

☆頭尾可打開、縮合。

⑫ 整理翅膀的形狀，即算完成

出的翅膀向箭頭…一邊也…

A hunter once caught a small bird. 'Master,' said the bird, 'you have eaten many animals bigger than me and they've not satisfied your appetite. How can the flesh of my tiny body fill you up? If you let me go, I'll teach you three secrets: one while I'm still in your hand, the second when I'm on top of your camouflage hat, and the third from the top of a tree. When you've heard these secrets, you'll consider yourself the luckiest hunter alive. The first secret is this: Don't believe the foolish pronouncements of others.'

The bird flew on to the hunter's hat, from where it gave the second secret: 'Don't have any regrets for what is past. Concealed in my body is a precious pearl weighing five ounces. It was yours by right, and now it's gone.'

Hearing this, the hunter began to wail and curse.

'What's up?' asked the bird. 'Didn't I just teach you not to have any regrets for the past? I also said, Don't believe the foolish things that people say. I weigh less than two ounces, so how could I possibly conceal a pearl weighing five?'

Coming to his senses, the hunter asked to be taught the third secret.

'Get real,' said the bird. 'Seeing how much notice you took of the first two secrets, why should I waste the third?'

How to Grill Chicken

Serves 2

- 2 chicken breasts
- 3–4 tablespoons of olive oil
- Juice of 1 lemon, or orange if
  you're feeling fruity
- 1–2 cloves of garlic
- Salt and black pepper

Place a piece of cling film over a large chopping board and place a chicken breast on top. Cover with another sheet of cling film.

Use a rolling pin to bang the chicken out flat, until it is almost transparent and approaching the size of the chopping board. Repeat with the other chicken breast.

Place the flattened chicken in a plastic box with the olive oil, citrus juice, garlic and salt and black pepper. Leave to marinate for at least 1 hour, or even overnight if you're very organised.

Take a bath with some rosemary sprigs in it – you'll come out feeling stimulated and smelling like a spring lamb.

This method of flattening (chefs call it battering) the fillets to make them cook quickly and evenly, leaves you more time to debate the clubbing / parenthood chicken / egg question.

When ready to cook, heat a chargrill pan until very hot, or overhead grill on the highest setting. Drain the chicken of its marinade.

Turn the heat under the pan down to medium and lay the chicken on the chargrill. Cook for 1 minute on each side.

Roasted Birds

ROASTED BIRDS

USE THE BEST BIRDS YOU CAN LAY HANDS ON. YOU KNOW THAT THE REARING OF BATTERY CHICKENS SHOULD NOT BE ENCOURAGED, SO SPEND THE EXTRA ON REAL FREE RANGE OR CONSERVATION BIRDS, OR (BEST OF ALL) BUY ORGANIC... AND LINE YOUR ROASTING TIN WITH A DOUBLE-THICKNESS OF FOIL, AS YOU HAVE BETTER THINGS TO DO THAN WASHING UP... RUB SOME OIL OVER THE FIRST PART OF THE BIRD TO BE IN CONTACT WITH THE FOIL TO STOP IT FROM STICKING.

AS YOU MAY REMEMBER, ROASTING (JUST LIKE YOUR SUMMER HOLIDAYS) IS THE ART OF HEAT, TIME AND MOISTURISING.

HEAT
DOMESTIC OVENS TEND TO GIVE INACCURATE TEMPERATURE READINGS, SO GET THE OVEN AS HOT AS IT WILL GO, WHACK THE BIRD IN, AND TURN THE HEAT DOWN TO MEDIUM OR HALF.

TIME
THERE ARE LOTS OF FASCINATING CHARTS THAT REQUIRE YOU TO WEIGH YOUR BIRD, DIVIDE IT BY THE CELSIUS EQUIVALENT AND CALCULATE THE TIME OF THE NEXT HIGH TIDE. HOWEVER, WHAT WE'RE DOING HERE IS NOT HOME ECONOMICS - WE'RE ARTISTS WITH FINELY TUNED INTUITION! CHECKING AND TURNING THE BIRD EVERY FIFTEEN MINUTES SO THAT IT CAN'T BE UNDER- OR OVER-DONE IS THE BEST SOLUTION, AND GIVES YOU TIME TO:

MOISTURISE
DON'T LET YOUR BIRD DRY OUT. SPOONFULS OF JUICES WILL FORM UNDERNEATH THE BIRD, AND THEY SHOULD BE SPOONED BACK OVER THE TOP OF WHICHEVER SIDE IS FACING UP AT THE TIME. TURNING AND MOISTURISING EVERY FIFTEEN MINUTES MEANS NO MORE DRY, STRINGY BIRDS. MOISTURISING WITH MELTED BUTTER GIVES A FLASHY, GOLDEN, MELTINGLY MOIST RESULT.

CHEFS SOMETIMES CHECK TO SEE IF A ROAST IS DONE BY STICKING A SKEWER INTO THE MEATIEST PART. IF IT COMES OUT CLEAN, THE MEAT SHOULD BE DONE; IF IT HAS SCRAPS OF MEAT ATTACHED, KEEP ON COOKING. MOST BIRDS COOK IN ABOUT 45 MINUTES, LESS FOR SMALL ONES, LONGER FOR LARGER ONES. THE TRICK IS TO THEN LET THE BIRD REST IN THE TIN AND OUT OF THE OVEN FOR 10 MINUTES OR SO AS THIS SEEMS TO RELAX THE MEAT AND MAKE FOR BETTER CUTTING AND EATING...

DO TURKEYS SEEM WORTH IT TO YOU? THEY'RE HARD TO COOK, UNLESS YOU HAVE A HUGE OVEN AND BICEPS TO MATCH, AND EVEN THE BEST ONES AMONG THEM, SUCH AS THE ORGANIC BRONZE VARIETY, CAN BE TOO MUCH TO DEAL WITH... AT FESTIVE TIMES, DON'T YOU PREFER TO DO CHICKEN WITH A GRAND ACCOMPANIMENT TO CELEBRATE THE OCCASION? REAL TRUFFLES COST LOADS, AND TRANSFORM THE EVERYDAY INTO THE SUBLIME. THEY ALSO SMELL OF SEX.

Chicken with Preserved Lemons and Caperberries

Serves 4

- 1.5kg chicken, jointed, skinned
- ½ small onion
- 3 tablespoons of olive oil
- ¼ teaspoon of turmeric
- 2 large potatoes
- 2 preserved lemons, or 2 fresh lemons, peeled and rolled in salt
- 150g caperberries
- A few sprigs of coriander
- Black pepper

Preserved lemons used to be available only from shops selling North African groceries, but the better supermarket chains are now stocking them. If you can't find them, or can't find the time to look, use fresh lemons. Peel them and roll them in salt, then follow the recipe and hope for the best.

Very North Africa, this. Put on a CD by Cheb Khaled, and sway sensually to those big Rai beats. Wear lots of dark eye-make-up and harem pants. Imagine the dense reek of hashish as it drifts from the bedroom of your lover, who is fantasising about you. Turn off the TV. Do not eat Fry's Turkish Delight as it will spoil your appetite.

Joint the chicken into 4 or 8 pieces. If you don't fancy doing that, buy chicken pieces or get the butcher to do your dirty work for you.

↓

Chop the onion. Heat the olive oil in a large flameproof casserole or heavy pot, add the onion and fry for 5 minutes or until softened.

↓

Add the turmeric, then turn the heat to medium-high and brown the chicken pieces all over. Add a few tablespoons of water if the mixture starts to scorch.

→ Meanwhile, boil some water and peel and quarter the potatoes. Cut the preserved lemons lengthways into eighths and rinse them thoroughly to remove some of the salty flavour.

↓

When the chicken and onions are brown, add 600ml of the boiling water to the casserole, then add the potatoes and lemons.

↓

Remove the stalks from the caperberries and slice them in half lengthways.

← Bring the mixture to the boil then lower the heat and leave to simmer for 45 minutes, uncovered.

↓

Bring a small saucepan of water to the boil, add the caperberries and simmer for 30 seconds. Drain and refresh under cold running water.

→ Check the chicken after it has been cooking for 45 minutes: if the pieces are on the larger size of small, it may need to cook for another 10–15 minutes. The flesh should be falling off the bone. The sauce should be salty, lemony and unctuous, but still quite liquid, and you might want to add some pepper.

↓

Paint henna patterns on your hands and feet using a doily and some cocoa powder paste. It'll look rubbish, but tomcats will like you.

When the chicken is nearly ready, add the caperberries and stir to combine. Cook for another 3–5 minutes.

↓

Serve, garnished with the coriander, in deep soup bowls.

Serving Option A

Serve with couscous.

Serving Option D

Serve with Persian Rice (see page 52).

Serving Option B

Serve with Smooth Chickpeas (see page 129).

Serving Option C

Serve with Donna Karan, if you know her well enough to invite round for a chicken supper.

Chicken with Preserved Lemons and Caperberries

Polo Zhereshk

👫👫/👫👫👫/👫👨

Serves 4 from Tehran,
6 from Qom, where they like to fast quite a lot,
or 3 from Merv

- 1 small chicken, jointed, skinned
- 2 tablespoons of olive oil
- 1½ tablespoons of butter
- 30g barberries or 150g cranberries
  (choose frozen, they're always
  about and they last well in the
  freezer for frozen Sea Breezes)
- A pinch of saffron threads
- 1 egg
- 500ml yoghurt
- Salt and black pepper

Here's a dish which should be made with tiny Iranian zhereshk or barberries, which are used for the sharp fruitiness that they impart to the dish. As it's hard to find these (unless you have an Iranian community nearby), cranberries are a great substitute, being sharp, fruit and fashionable.

The Thief

A MAN of Merv, well known as the home of complicated thinkers, ran shouting one night through the city's streets. 'Thief, Thief!' he cried.

The people surrounded him, and when he was a little calmer, asked: 'Where was the thief?'

'In my house.'

'Did you see him?'

'No.'

'Was anything missing?'

'No.'

'How do you know there was a thief then?'

'I was lying in bed when I remembered that thieves break into houses without a sound, and move very quietly. I could hear nothing, so I knew that there was a thief in the house, you fool!'

(*Niamat Khan*).

*   *   *

Know your measure.

Proverb.

Try to buy the chicken ready-skinned, but if you can't, remove the skin before cooking.

Heat the olive oil and butter in a flameproof casserole or heavy pot and, when the butter is foaming, add the chicken one or two pieces at a time and cook until brown on the outside and cooked in the middle. This will take about 20 minutes. Stick a knife into the flesh. If the juices run clear, your chicken is cooked.

When the chicken is cooked, remove it from the heat and leave it to cool.

Meanwhile, if using barberries, place them in a small saucepan, cover with water and set over a medium-high heat. Bring to the boil and cook for 1 minute or so until soft, then leave them to drain.

Alternatively, if you're using cranberries, let them defrost.

Place the saffron threads in a small cup and cover with about 2 tablespoons of boiling water. Leave to steep for 10 minutes.

Heat the oven to 180°C/350°F/Gas Mark 4. In a large bowl, beat the egg, then stir in the yoghurt and the saffron liquid.

When the chicken is cool, remove it from the bone, cut the flesh into strips as wide as your finger, and add it to the yoghurt mixture in the bowl. Stir in the fruit and season to taste.

Transfer the mixture to an ovenproof dish and bake for 20–30 minutes or until heated through. Serve with rice and a feeling of elation.

Alternatively, add the mixture to an equal weight of Persian Rice (see page 52), and bake for 20–30 minutes until heated through. In which case, serve wearing unbleached linen, quoting Omar Khayam.

Coq au Vin

👨👩👨👩

Serves 4

- 3 tablespoons of olive oil
- 8 chicken drumsticks, or 4 leg
  and thigh chicken portions
- 1 onion
- 200g mushrooms
- 12 cloves of garlic
- 750ml (1 bottle) red country wine
- 2 tablespoons of butter
- Salt and black pepper
- 6 shallots
- 150g crème fraîche

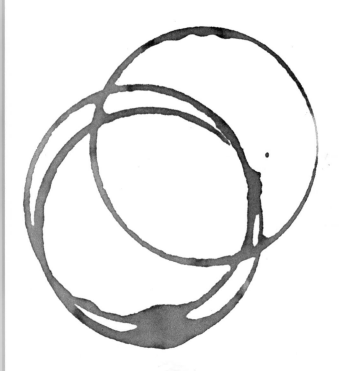

This recipe is more fun to make, and will be given
a more authentic French feel if you drink half the
wine you're supposed to be cooking with.

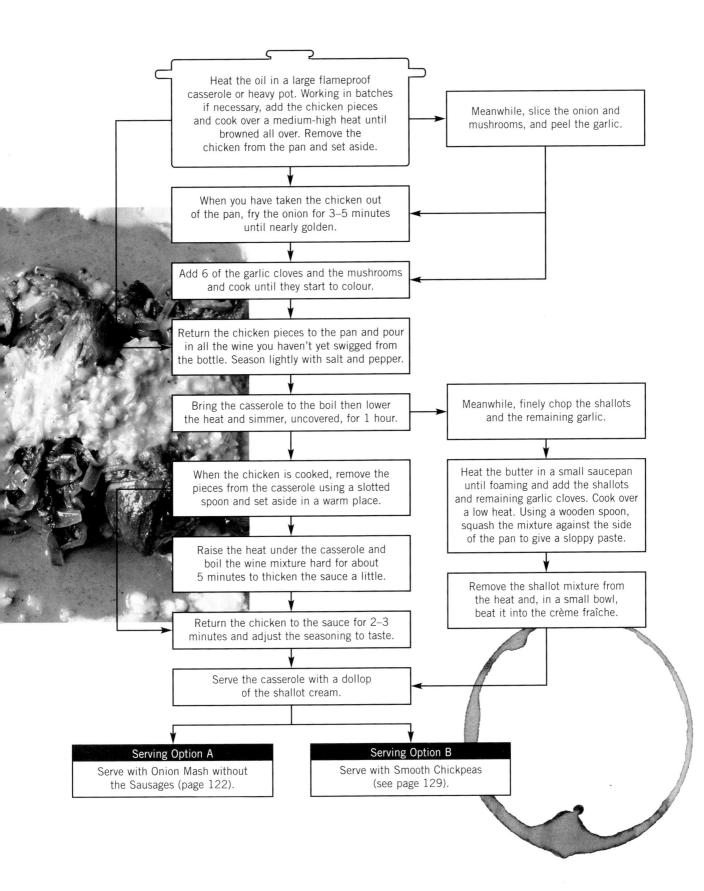

Heat the oil in a large flameproof casserole or heavy pot. Working in batches if necessary, add the chicken pieces and cook over a medium-high heat until browned all over. Remove the chicken from the pan and set aside.

Meanwhile, slice the onion and mushrooms, and peel the garlic.

When you have taken the chicken out of the pan, fry the onion for 3–5 minutes until nearly golden.

Add 6 of the garlic cloves and the mushrooms and cook until they start to colour.

Return the chicken pieces to the pan and pour in all the wine you haven't yet swigged from the bottle. Season lightly with salt and pepper.

Bring the casserole to the boil then lower the heat and simmer, uncovered, for 1 hour.

Meanwhile, finely chop the shallots and the remaining garlic.

When the chicken is cooked, remove the pieces from the casserole using a slotted spoon and set aside in a warm place.

Heat the butter in a small saucepan until foaming and add the shallots and remaining garlic cloves. Cook over a low heat. Using a wooden spoon, squash the mixture against the side of the pan to give a sloppy paste.

Raise the heat under the casserole and boil the wine mixture hard for about 5 minutes to thicken the sauce a little.

Remove the shallot mixture from the heat and, in a small bowl, beat it into the crème fraîche.

Return the chicken to the sauce for 2–3 minutes and adjust the seasoning to taste.

Serve the casserole with a dollop of the shallot cream.

Serving Option A
Serve with Onion Mash without the Sausages (page 122).

Serving Option B
Serve with Smooth Chickpeas (see page 129).

Chicken and Walnut Salad

Serves 4

- 4 chicken breasts
- A few strips of lemon peel
- A few strips of orange peel
- A handful of peppercorns
- 120g walnuts, or pecans, or hazelnuts
- A large handful of wild or regular rocket
- 225ml good-quality mayonnaise
- Salt and black pepper

AT LEAST THAT ANSWERS THE QUESTION!

In a large frying pan, place the chicken pieces, citrus peel and peppercorns and cover with water. Set over a medium-high heat and bring to the boil, then lower the heat and simmer gently for 25 minutes.

Meanwhile, in a small frying pan, toast the nuts until fragrant and lightly browned, then set aside to cool.

Remove the chicken from the liquid and set aside to cool thoroughly.

Finely chop half the rocket and leave the rest as whole leaves, removing any stalks as necessary.

Coarsely chop the nuts when they have cooled.

Place the mayonnaise in a large bowl. Cut the chicken into strips and add it to the mayonnaise along with the chopped rocket. Stir thoroughly and season to taste.

Serving Option A

Stir through the whole rocket leaves and the nuts just before serving.

Serving Option B

Stir the nuts into the chicken mayonnaise, then serve the mixture on a bed of the whole rocket leaves.

Soft-Boiled Chicken

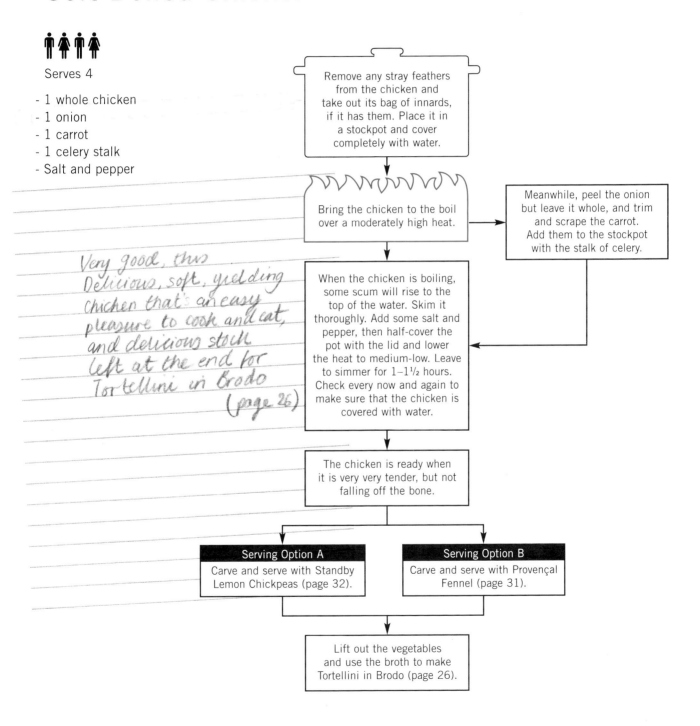

Serves 4

- 1 whole chicken
- 1 onion
- 1 carrot
- 1 celery stalk
- Salt and pepper

Remove any stray feathers from the chicken and take out its bag of innards, if it has them. Place it in a stockpot and cover completely with water.

Bring the chicken to the boil over a moderately high heat.

Meanwhile, peel the onion but leave it whole, and trim and scrape the carrot. Add them to the stockpot with the stalk of celery.

When the chicken is boiling, some scum will rise to the top of the water. Skim it thoroughly. Add some salt and pepper, then half-cover the pot with the lid and lower the heat to medium-low. Leave to simmer for 1–1½ hours. Check every now and again to make sure that the chicken is covered with water.

The chicken is ready when it is very very tender, but not falling off the bone.

Serving Option A
Carve and serve with Standby Lemon Chickpeas (page 32).

Serving Option B
Carve and serve with Provençal Fennel (page 31).

Lift out the vegetables and use the broth to make Tortellini in Brodo (page 26).

Very good, this
Delicious, soft, yielding
chicken that's an easy
pleasure to cook and eat,
and delicious stock
left at the end for
Tortellini in Brodo
(page 26)

Duck Breasts with Balsamic Vinegar

Chicken with Sweet Peppers

Serves 4

- 1 onion
- 2 cloves of garlic
- 2 tablespoons of olive oil
- 1 chicken, jointed and skinned
- 3 red and yellow sweet peppers
- Salt and black pepper
- A few sprigs of fresh marjoram
  or oregano

This is the perfect partner to Earth
Wind and Fire. Do you remember?
When it was time? September!

Chop the onion and slice
the garlic. Heat the olive
oil in a flameproof casserole
or stockpot and fry the
onion over a moderate heat
until transparent.

Add the garlic and after
about 30 seconds, when
it's fragrant, add the chicken
and brown it all over.

Meanwhile, cut the sweet
peppers into strips, binning
the core and seeds. When
the chicken is browned, rinse
the strips of pepper under the
tap and add them to the
casserole without letting them
dry. Season with salt and
pepper and stir to combine.

Lower the heat right down,
cover and leave to cook for
20 minutes until the strips of
pepper are quite soft and a
little clear gravy has formed.

Pick the leaves from the
herb sprigs and add them
to the pan. Stir, then cover
and continue cooking for
another 10 minutes or until
the chicken is tender and
cooked right through.

Serving Option A
Serve with plain boiled
new potatoes.

Serving Option B
Serve with Baked Potatoes
(see page 34).

Duck Breasts with Balsamic Vinegar

Serves 4

- 2 tablespoons of sunflower or other clear oil
- 4 duck breast fillets
- 120ml/8 tablespoons of cheap balsamic vinegar
- 2 handfuls (1 large mugful) of frozen cranberries or green seedless grapes
- Salt and black pepper

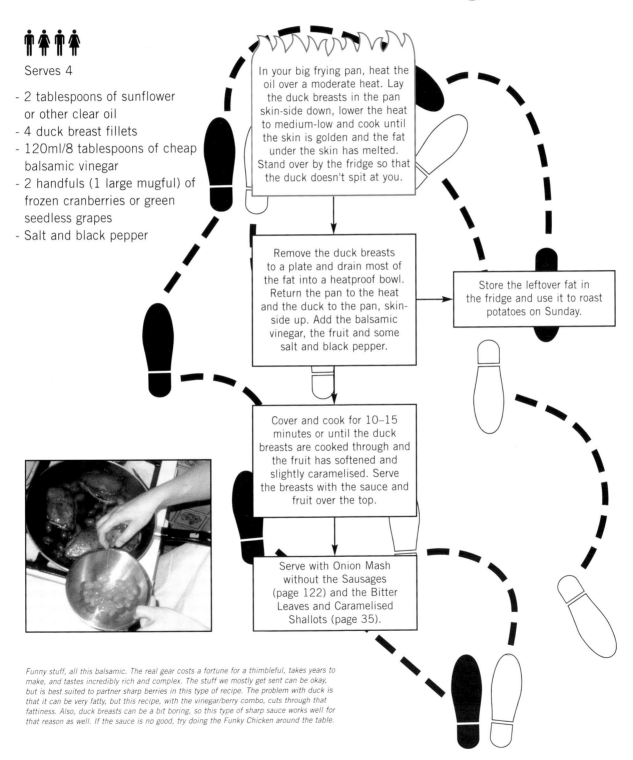

In your big frying pan, heat the oil over a moderate heat. Lay the duck breasts in the pan skin-side down, lower the heat to medium-low and cook until the skin is golden and the fat under the skin has melted. Stand over by the fridge so that the duck doesn't spit at you.

Remove the duck breasts to a plate and drain most of the fat into a heatproof bowl. Return the pan to the heat and the duck to the pan, skin-side up. Add the balsamic vinegar, the fruit and some salt and black pepper.

Store the leftover fat in the fridge and use it to roast potatoes on Sunday.

Cover and cook for 10–15 minutes or until the duck breasts are cooked through and the fruit has softened and slightly caramelised. Serve the breasts with the sauce and fruit over the top.

Serve with Onion Mash without the Sausages (page 122) and the Bitter Leaves and Caramelised Shallots (page 35).

Funny stuff, all this balsamic. The real gear costs a fortune for a thimbleful, takes years to make, and tastes incredibly rich and complex. The stuff we mostly get sent can be okay, but is best suited to partner sharp berries in this type of recipe. The problem with duck is that it can be very fatty, but this recipe, with the vinegar/berry combo, cuts through that fattiness. Also, duck breasts can be a bit boring, so this type of sharp sauce works well for that reason as well. If the sauce is no good, try doing the Funky Chicken around the table.

Whole Roast Duck with Hairdryer

Serves 4

- 1 small duck
- 1 onion
- A small handful of Maldon Sea salt
- 1 hairdryer
- 1 packet of marigolds

Fill a large pot about three-quarters full of water and bring it to the boil.

Remove the bags of innards from the duck. Prick the duck all over with a fork.

Place the duck in the boiling water and simmer for 15 minutes, making sure the duck is covered with water.

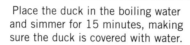

Drain the duck.

Plug in a hairdryer and put on some rubber gloves. Stick one hand up the duck's arse and, working over the sink or the pot you've just boiled the duck in, blow-dry the duck on the highest setting for 15 minutes. The layer of fat underneath the skin should melt and drip out of the holes.

Heat the oven to 200°C/400°F/ Gas Mark 6. Peel the onion and place it inside the cavity, cutting the onion in half if necessary.

Rub the salt all over the skin, then roast for 45 minutes, basting every 15 minutes or so with some of the juices that have formed in the bottom of the roasting pan.

Serve with Butter Baked Witloof (page 39), having first removed the rubber gloves, silly.

This is an echo of the Chinese wind-dried method: ducks are delicious to eat but have a thick layer of fat between skin and flesh that can be a bit off-putting. In this dish, the boiling step enlarges the pores, where the feathers used to be. This means that the heat from the hairdryer melts that layer of fat, causing it to drip out of the newly-big pores, and allows the cooked duck to have a puffed-up crispy skin. Please note that a nozzle-free hairdryer produces the best results. Big Hair diffusers do not give ducks big skin. Oh, and wear rubber gloves while blow-drying to avoid nasty shocks.

Goose with Curling Tongs and Crimpers

There is no such dish.

Aberdeen Angus
top rump

for roasting

From farms mee   British
farm   dards

£8.49
kg

£3.85
lb

Aberdeen A...
topside cor...

For roas...
From farms meeting the Briti...
farm assured standar...

Eating meat as a condim
than the main part of a
Quality is the key, so spe
and with the better taste
happy, and satisfied with

ent or flavouring, rather
dish, is the smartest way.
nd more, buy organic,
and texture you'll be
less.

How to Grill Meat

Serves 2

- 1–2 tablespoons of olive oil
- A splash of vinegar or lemon juice
- 1 clove of garlic
- 2 beef steaks, sirloin or rump
- Salt
- Cling film

Sirloin steak is soft and nice.
Rump steak's chewier,
but has the best flavour.
Fillet steak is the softest of the lot,
but has the least flavour and costs the most.
So make your choice.
Bernie the Bolt, please.

Place the oil and vinegar or lemon juice in a mister (see page 121), adding more as required to get the pump action working.

Crush the garlic with the flat blade of a knife and add it to the mister with a generous pinch of salt. Set aside for the flavours to meld.

Place a sheet of cling film over a large cutting board and lay a steak on top of it. Cover with another sheet of cling film.

Using a mallet or rolling pin, and working from the centre outwards, bash the steak out until it is as large and as uniformly thin as possible.

Heat a chargrill pan or overhead grill on the highest setting.

Using the mister, spray the oil mixture over both sides of the meat.

If using a chargrill, turn the heat down to medium then place the steak on the chargrill. Cook for 1 minute on each side.

If using an overhead grill, cook the meat 5–8cm away from the heat source for 1–2 minutes on each side.

Stick the end of a sharp knife in the steak: it is not yet cooked if the meat oozes bright red juices or the knife is coated with bits of meat when removed. If you like rare meat, wait till a stuck piece of steak oozes pinky juice.

Lancashire Hot Pot

Serves 4

- 500g stewing lamb
- 4–5 large potatoes
- 4 large carrots
- 2–3 tablespoons of cooking oil
- About 300ml of Boddington's Bitter
- Salt and black pepper

Ritual for its own sake

A missionary who had been captured by cannibals was sitting in a cooking-pot of rapidly heating water when he saw the cannibals with their hands clasped in prayer. He said to the nearest one: "So you are devout Christians?"

"Not only am I a Christian", replied the annoyed cannibal, "but I strongly object to being interrupted while saying grace!"

Reprinted by permission from *Special Illumination*, by Idries Shah (Octagon Press Ltd, London).

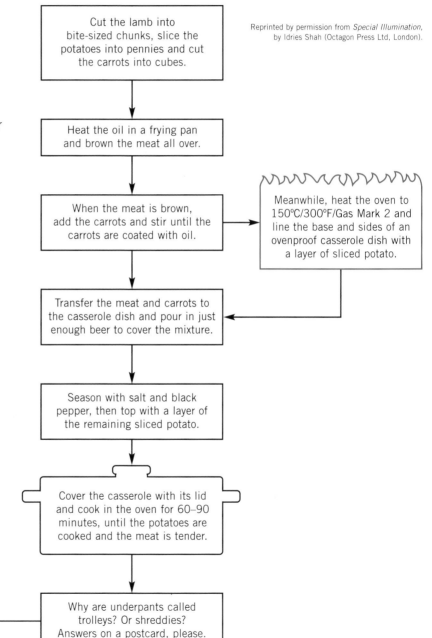

Cut the lamb into bite-sized chunks, slice the potatoes into pennies and cut the carrots into cubes.

↓

Heat the oil in a frying pan and brown the meat all over.

↓

When the meat is brown, add the carrots and stir until the carrots are coated with oil.

→ Meanwhile, heat the oven to 150°C/300°F/Gas Mark 2 and line the base and sides of an ovenproof casserole dish with a layer of sliced potato.

↓

Transfer the meat and carrots to the casserole dish and pour in just enough beer to cover the mixture.

↓

Season with salt and black pepper, then top with a layer of the remaining sliced potato.

↓

Cover the casserole with its lid and cook in the oven for 60–90 minutes, until the potatoes are cooked and the meat is tender.

↓

Why are underpants called trolleys? Or shreddies? Answers on a postcard, please.

Meatballs with Flatbread and Yoghurt Sauce

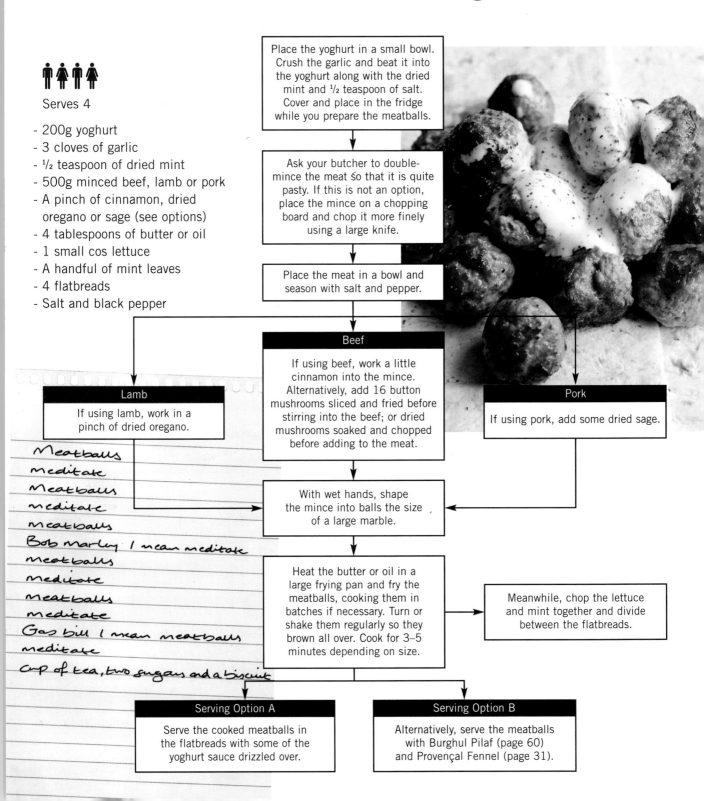

Serves 4

- 200g yoghurt
- 3 cloves of garlic
- ½ teaspoon of dried mint
- 500g minced beef, lamb or pork
- A pinch of cinnamon, dried oregano or sage (see options)
- 4 tablespoons of butter or oil
- 1 small cos lettuce
- A handful of mint leaves
- 4 flatbreads
- Salt and black pepper

Place the yoghurt in a small bowl. Crush the garlic and beat it into the yoghurt along with the dried mint and ½ teaspoon of salt. Cover and place in the fridge while you prepare the meatballs.

Ask your butcher to double-mince the meat so that it is quite pasty. If this is not an option, place the mince on a chopping board and chop it more finely using a large knife.

Place the meat in a bowl and season with salt and pepper.

Beef

If using beef, work a little cinnamon into the mince. Alternatively, add 16 button mushrooms sliced and fried before stirring into the beef; or dried mushrooms soaked and chopped before adding to the meat.

Lamb

If using lamb, work in a pinch of dried oregano.

Pork

If using pork, add some dried sage.

With wet hands, shape the mince into balls the size of a large marble.

Heat the butter or oil in a large frying pan and fry the meatballs, cooking them in batches if necessary. Turn or shake them regularly so they brown all over. Cook for 3–5 minutes depending on size.

Meanwhile, chop the lettuce and mint together and divide between the flatbreads.

Serving Option A

Serve the cooked meatballs in the flatbreads with some of the yoghurt sauce drizzled over.

Serving Option B

Alternatively, serve the meatballs with Burghul Pilaf (page 60) and Provençal Fennel (page 31).

Handwritten note in margin:
Meatballs
meditate
Meatballs
meditate
meatballs
Bob Marley I mean meditate
meatballs
meditate
meatballs
meditate
Gas bill I mean meatballs
meditate
cup of tea, two sugars and a biscuit

Roast Lamb with Potatoes, Artichokes and Oregano

Serves 4

- 1kg potatoes, preferably yellow-skinned mids
- 4–6 large Jerusalem artichokes
- 1 small leg of lamb
- A handful of garlic cloves
- A little oil or butter
- 1 tablespoon of fresh oregano leaves
- About 350ml red wine
- About 350ml stock (see pages 152–153)
- Cooking foil, with butter thinly smeared on one side

Peel the potatoes and slice them about 5mm thick.

Place the potatoes in a large saucepan, cover with water and bring to the boil. Simmer for 5 minutes, then drain.

Using the large knife, cut slashes across the top of the lamb joint. Cut the garlic into slivers and insert them under the skin of the meat.

Heat the oven to 200°C/400°F/Gas Mark 6. Line your roasting tin with kitchen foil, then grease with some oil or butter.

Meanwhile, peel the Jerusalem artichokes, and cut into equal slices as thick as a CD cover.

Place a layer of the parboiled potatoes in the base of the roasting tin, then cover with a layer of sliced artichokes.

Cover with the remaining potato then sprinkle with the oregano.

Pour in the red wine and stock – you want just enough liquid to cover the tops of the vegetables; add some water if necessary.

Sit the lamb on top of the vegetables and cover the tin with a sheet of greased kitchen foil.

Roast the lamb for 40 minutes, then remove the top layer of foil, baste the lamb and continue cooking uncovered for another 30 minutes.

Check the lamb again and cook for another 10–20 minutes, checking every 10 minutes or so to see if the lamb is ready by sticking the point of a knife in as far as you can. If it comes out with bits of meat still stuck to the blade, keep cooking. If loads of bloody juice oozes out and you like your meat well done, keep cooking.

When ready, remove from the oven and leave to stand for 10–15 minutes before serving, to relax the meat.

Serve at the table, giving each guest a portion of the potato and artichoke cake as well as some of the winey gravy.

Roast Lamb with Potatoes, Artichokes and Oregano

Steak Sandwich with Pesto or Mustard

Serves 2 (after the football)

- 1–2 tablespoons of olive oil
- A splash of vinegar or lemon juice
- 1 clove of garlic
- Salt
- 2 beef steaks
- 4 slices of bread
- 2–3 tablespoons of fresh basil
  pesto or French mustard

We're in the last minute of full time, and it's Beckham with the corner, Schmeichel's gone up from his goal into the opposition's penalty area – he manages to get a head on it towards Sheringham, who hits it and it's in the net!! Bayern don't believe it – Manchester United have equalised in the last minute of full time!! What an amazing turn about, and in the last minute of this Champion's League final. The United fans are going mental!

Bayern take the kick-off, looking frankly, dispirited and United have the ball again! It's Beckham, who's been tireless in central midfield, a long, raking pass to Giggs – Giggs takes the ball all the way down the right wing to the by-line, and wins a corner from the Bayern defender, who looks like he's had all the fight knocked out of him.

We're in injury time here at the Nou Camp Stadium, as David Beckham takes what must be the final corner of this period. He hits a fast, viciously curling ball which is won by Sheringham, who knocks it down to Solskjaer, who side-foots it INTO THE TOP OF THE NET!!!!

I DON'T BELIEVE IT!!!!
SOLSKJAER WHEELS AWAY, IS MOBBED BY HIS TEAM-MATES.
THE BAYERN PLAYERS ARE ON THE GROUND, THEIR NUMBER 4 IS OPENLY WEEPING, THERE'S PANDEMONIUM ON THE TERRACES!!!!!

You can always put a mister to good use around the kitchen. Fill him with oil, and spray your pan with an even coat before frying. Salad dressings work well in misters, too, allowing you to spritz salads lightly but thoroughly before serving. Trigger-happy DISHY people know that their mister works particularly well when full of alcohol, turning ice cream, fresh fruit and fruit salads from straight desserts into very DISHY ones!

Place the oil and vinegar or lemon juice in a mister, adding more as necessary to get the pump action working.

Crush the garlic and add it to the mister with a generous pinch of salt. Set aside for the flavours to meld.

Lay a sheet of cling film over a large cutting board and lay a steak on top of it. Cover with another sheet of cling film.

Using a mallet or rolling pin, bash the steak out until it is as large and as uniformly thin as possible.

Heat an overhead grill on the highest setting and toast the bread on one side only.

Spray the oil mixture over both sides of the meat.

Cook the meat 5–8cm away from the heat source for 1–2 minutes on each side. Stick the end of a sharp knife in the steak: it is not yet cooked if the meat oozes red juices or the knife is coated with bits of meat when removed.

Meanwhile, spread the ungrilled side of the bread with the pesto or mustard.

When the steaks are cooked, place each on a slice of bread and top with the remaining bread.

Press down hard on the sandwiches with the heel of your hand, then cut them into triangles and eat immediately.

Sausages with Onion Mash

👨👩👨👩

Serves 4

- 3 onions
- 3 tablespoons of olive oil
- 8–12 natural-skinned sausages
- 4 tablespoons of balsamic or
  sherry vinegar

For the mash:
- 6 floury old potatoes
- About 300ml milk
- A small tub of cream, if you
  think your arteries are up to it
- As much butter as you dare
- Salt and black pepper

Only attempt to do this with proper sausages. Do not accept sausages that are less than all meat, or have cereal fillers or artificial preservatives. Real people take time to roast sausages because that makes them taste richer and more savoury. The tantalising smell coming from the oven can be a powerful come-on, and the extra time the sausages take to cook can be used to make the onion mash.

Place a roasting tin in the oven and heat the oven to 200°C/400°F/Gas Mark 6.

Meanwhile, slice the onions. Heat the olive oil in a frying pan and sauté the onions until translucent.

Remove the hot roasting tin from the oven and transfer half the onions from the frying pan to the roasting tin. Set the frying pan aside until later.

Add the sausages to the roasting tin and stir until they are well coated with the onions.

Meanwhile, to make the mash, place the potatoes in a large saucepan or pot, cover with salted water and bring to the boil. Simmer until the potatoes are cooked through – they will be tender when pierced with a fork or skewer.

Place in the oven for 40 minutes, turning occasionally to brown the sausages all over.

Meanwhile, set the frying pan back over a medium heat and continue to cook the remaining onions, stirring constantly, until caramelised and toffee-coloured. Set aside.

Drain the potatoes under cold running water and leave them until cool enough to handle.

Burning your hands, peel the cooled potatoes and place the potato flesh back in the saucepan or pot. Add the milk and butter and do the mashed potato.

Mash the potatoes with a fork or potato masher, using a lifting, circular motion to incorporate as much air as possible into the mixture. If you're adding cream, do it now.

Stir the caramelised onions into the mash. Taste it. Does it need more salt? Or pepper? Or butter? Transfer to a serving platter or individual plates and set aside in a warm place.

When the sausages are done, remove them from the oven and put them and their onion coating on top of the mash.

Place the roasting tin over a medium heat and add the vinegar. Stir vigorously with a wooden spoon to incorporate the caramelised cooking juices into the liquid. This is what celebrity chefs call deglazing the pan, but what do they know?

Alternatively, you can make the dish in advance. To reheat, cover with foil and place in a 200°C/400°F/Gas Mark 6 oven for 15–20 minutes.

Pour the pan juices over the sausages and mash and serve immediately.

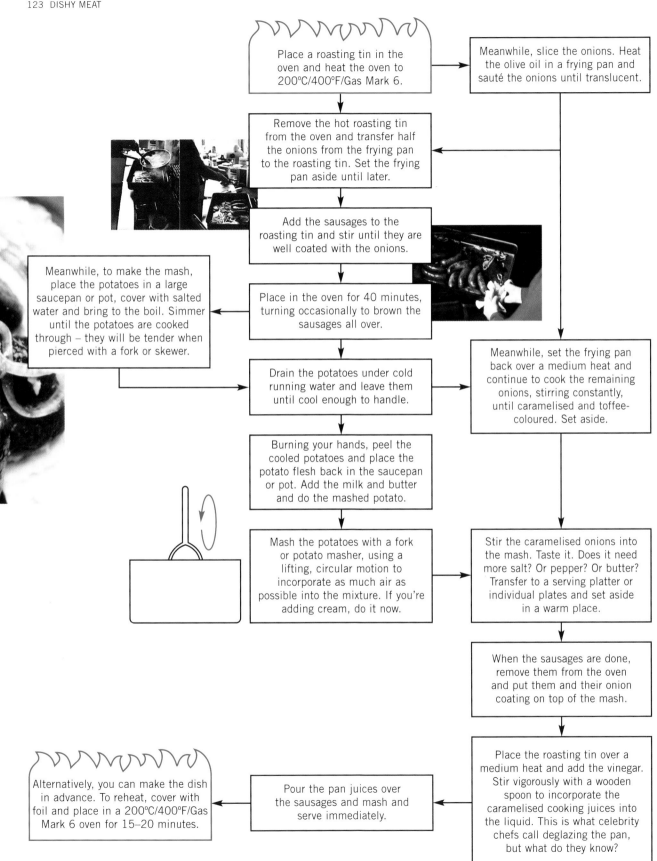

Venice Calves' Liver

Serves 2 (if you get lucky)

- 2 medium onions
- 1 tablespoon of oil
- 1 tablespoon of butter
- 250g calves' liver
- A little flour
- Salt and black pepper
- 2 tablespoons of balsamic vinegar
- A squeeze of lemon

Thinly slice the onions. Heat the oil and butter in a large frying pan and sauté the onions over a low heat until floppy but not coloured.

Meanwhile, cut the liver into 1cm wide strips.

Set the onions aside on a serving dish, cover with foil and keep in a warm place.

Sieve a little flour on to a work surface and season with salt and pepper. Roll the strips of liver in the flour until evenly coated.

Return the frying pan to the heat and add a little extra oil and butter if it looks a bit dry.

Cook the liver quickly over a high heat for 30–45 seconds, then transfer to the dish of onions.

Lower the heat to medium-low. Add the vinegar and lemon juice to the frying pan and stir vigorously with a wooden spoon to scrape up the caramelised cooking juices.

Pour the pan juices over the liver and serve immediately.

Venice is really known for its fish and seafood, which is unsurprising given its watery aspect. But Venetians love offal, and this version of Fegato alla Veneziana with its soft sweet onions might give you a clue why.

Serving Option A
Garnish with wedges of lemon if you like, dipping them in some finely-chopped parsley if you're trying to impress someone.

Serving Option B
This is good served with Onion Mash without the Onions (page 122).

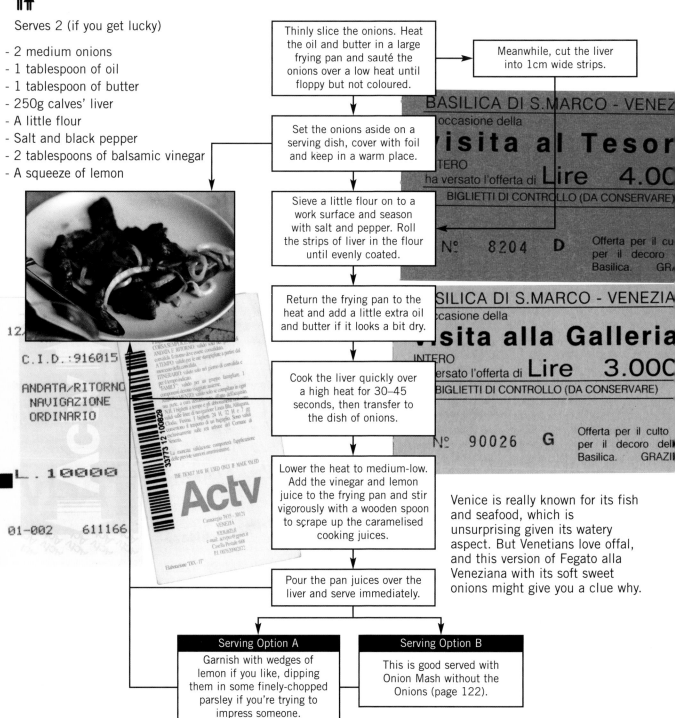

Lambs' Kidney Sandwich with Shredded Cabbage and Sumac

Serves 2

- 2 lambs' kidneys
- ½ lemon
- 1 small wedge red cabbage, about the diameter of your pitta bread
- 1 small wedge white cabbage, same sort of size
- 2 teaspoons of olive oil
- 1–2 tablespoons of butter
- 2 pitta breads
- ½ teaspoon of sumac or hot paprika
- Salt and black pepper

Buy the kidneys ready-cleaned by the butcher. Slice them as thinly as possible, removing the core as necessary, and place in a small bowl of water acidulated with a squeeze of lemon juice – the kidneys will go a little grey.

↓

Finely shred the cabbage – you will need a handful of each. Place in a bowl and toss with the olive oil and 1 teaspoon of juice from the lemon.

↓

Heat the butter in a frying pan. Drain the kidneys then sauté them in the butter, adding some freshly ground black pepper.

→

Meanwhile, score a semicircle around the top end of each pitta bread, then splash them with a few drops of water from the tap and stick them in the toaster for about 30 seconds to warm them through.

↓

Scalding your fingers, open the pitta breads using the scored semicircle to form a pocket.

↓

Stuff the cabbage mixture and slivers of kidney inside the pitta breads then sprinkle with the sumac or hot paprika and a squeeze of lemon.

↓

Serve hot in a napkin without delay, and don't talk with your mouth full, it's rude.

This light lunch or supper dish makes a good talking point, and confirms you as an interesting, well-travelled, adventurous type.

The first time you tried sumac might have been when you were travelling on the way to Isfahan in Iran to visit the beautiful ninth-century arched bridge. Sumac was the reddy-brown coarse powder, made from crushed dried berries, with the sour-ish lemony taste that you sprinkled over your rice.

Lambs' Kidney Sandwich with Shredded Cabbage and Sumac

Burgers

Serves 2, before or after the cinema

- 250g best lean minced beef,
  or chuck steak if it's available
- 1–2 teaspoons of parsley leaves
- 2 small ice cubes, or pats of butter
  that you've stuck in the freezer for
  about an hour or so
- A dollop of American mustard

Have your butcher mince the beef twice if possible. Otherwise, place the meat on a chopping board and chop it more finely using a large knife.

↓

Finely chop the parsley and stir it into the minced beef.

↓

Using wet hands, shape the mince into patties.

↓

Make a hole with your finger in each burger and secrete an ice cube or pat of frozen butter in the centre, covering it back up with mince.

Heat a chargrill or barbecue to a high temperature. When hot, lower the heat to medium if possible and cook the burgers for 4–5 minutes on each side – the frozen cube in the centre will keep the interior pink and moist.

Alternatively, cook under an overhead grill, keeping the heat at the highest setting and placing the burgers 5–8cm away from the heat source.

↓

Serve with a dollop of American mustard and, if you like, the Sort of German Marinated Potato Salad with Red Onion Dressing (page 33) and Grated Carrot, Pine Nut and Orange Blossom Salad (page 38).

This is how smart Americans grill their burgers - the frozen centre keeps the middle moist while the meat's cooking.

Lamb Cutlets with Smooth Chickpeas

Serves 4

- 8 lamb cutlets
- A bunch of parsley
- A few sprigs of mint

For the chickpea purée:
- 2 x 400g canned chickpeas
- 3 cloves of garlic
- A sprig of rosemary
- Salt and black pepper

To Overhead Grill

Heat an overhead grill to the highest setting. Trim the cutlets of as much fat as you like, and place them on the grill rack, setting it 5–8cm away from the heat source.

To Chargrill

Heat a chargrill pan until very hot. Put the cutlets on the pan, and turn the heat down to medium. Grill for about 3 minutes on each side.

For the Purée

To make the chickpea purée, drain the cans of chickpeas and place them in a saucepan with fresh water to cover. Halve the garlic cloves and add them to the pan with the rosemary.

Bring to the boil, then lower the heat and simmer for 10 minutes.

Remove and discard the rosemary sprig, then drain the chickpeas, reserving the cooking water.

Either

Place the chickpeas in a bowl and mash with a fork until smooth, adding just enough of the reserved cooking water to make a thick purée.

Or

Place the chickpeas in a food processor and whizz until smooth, adding just enough of the reserved cooking water to make a thick purée.

Season the mixture to taste with salt and black pepper and set aside.

Grill the cutlets for approximately 3 minutes on each side.

Meanwhile, finely chop the parsley and mint together and place them on a saucer.

When the lamb is cooked, dip the meat part of each cutlet in the chopped herbs to coat on both sides.

Serve over the chickpea purée.

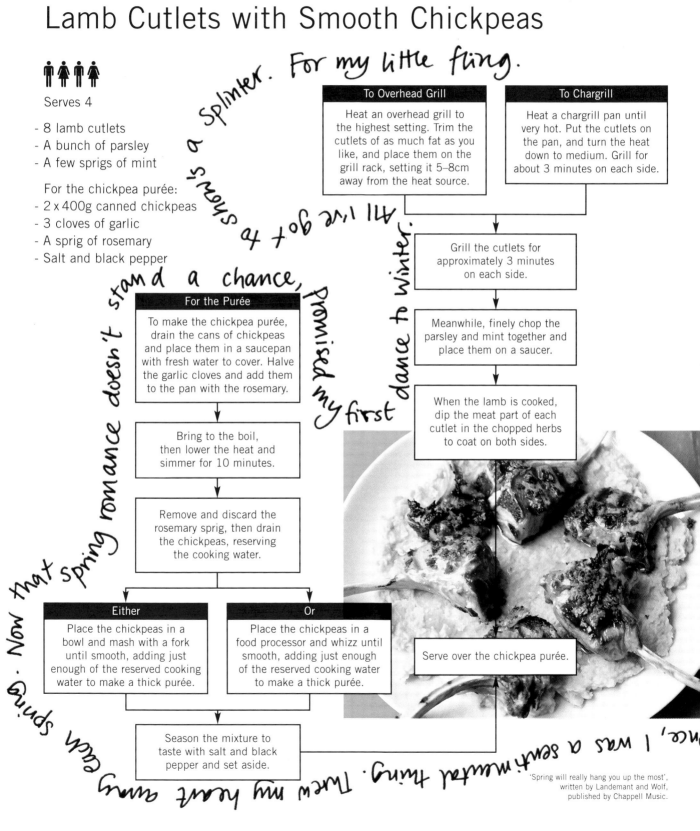

Handwritten: For my little fling. All I've got to show's a Splinter. Now that spring romance doesn't stand a chance, Promised my first dance to winter. Threw my heart away each spring. Since I was a sentimental thing.

'Spring will really hang you up the most', written by Landemant and Wolf, published by Chappell Music.

Misted Fresh Fruit

Serves 4

- About 4 tablespoons of alcohol, such as eau de vie, gin or vodka or about 8 tablespoons of orange blossom or rose water or about 8 tablespoons of herb tisane (page 173)
- About 1–1.5kg good-looking, eat-with-your-fingers fresh fruit, such as apricots, large berries, cherries, grapes, nectarines, oranges or peaches

Option A

Put the alcohol, flower water or herb tisane (see page 173) in a mister and place it in the freezer for 30–60 minutes to get really cold.

Just before serving, arrange the fruit on a platter, making sure it looks arty and interesting.

Mist the iced liquid over the fruit to give it a nice bloom, then serve with a winning smile.

Talk about Matisse and his contribution to the appreciation of twentieth-century nude.

CHARMS NOT WORKING FAST ENOUGH?

CONVERSATION FALTERING?

TIME RUNNING OUT ON YOU?

MIST FRESH FRUIT AND BERRIES LIKE THIS AND WATCH THOSE BARRIERS COME DOWN!

Fruit Salad with Mint Leaves

Serves 4

- About 1–1.5kg of fresh fruit, but not banana, because it goes brown
- 1 lemon, or 4 tablespoons of orange juice
- A small handful of mint leaves
- Maybe a bit of sugar or runny honey
- 2 teaspoons of strong alcohol, such as Armagnac or Maraschino if you fancy

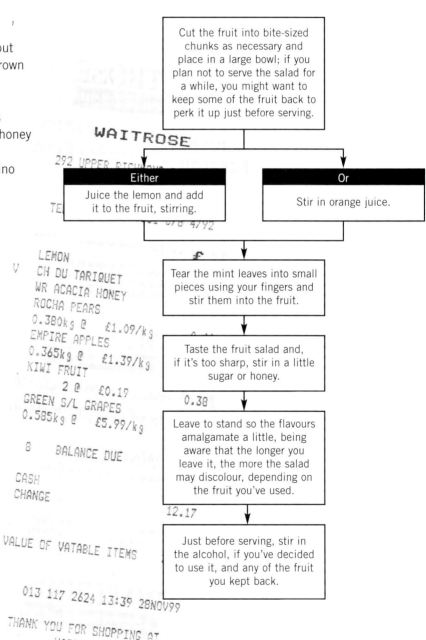

Cut the fruit into bite-sized chunks as necessary and place in a large bowl; if you plan not to serve the salad for a while, you might want to keep some of the fruit back to perk it up just before serving.

Either
Juice the lemon and add it to the fruit, stirring.

Or
Stir in orange juice.

Tear the mint leaves into small pieces using your fingers and stir them into the fruit.

Taste the fruit salad and, if it's too sharp, stir in a little sugar or honey.

Leave to stand so the flavours amalgamate a little, being aware that the longer you leave it, the more the salad may discolour, depending on the fruit you've used.

Just before serving, stir in the alcohol, if you've decided to use it, and any of the fruit you kept back.

Fruit Salad with Mint Leaves

Vegetable Stock

Makes 350–500ml

- 1 onion
- 1 carrot
- Other fresh or tired vegetables,
  but avoid cabbage, potato
  or tomato
- A few cloves of garlic
- A few stalks of parsley
- 1 bay leaf
- Salt

In an ideal world, we'd all be doing what's known as circular cooking, where the scraps, peelings and leftovers of today's dishes become stocks, soups and supper dishes for tomorrow. Of course, for this to happen, we'd have to be doing substantial kitchen work every day, and that's not necessarily what we're about. However, it makes sense, for instance, if you're roasting a chicken (page 93) or duck (page 108), to turn the carcass into a stock that'll last a week or so in the fridge. The same's true for all your vegetable peelings, whereby saving them in a plastic bag or bowl, they can be turned into stock while you're eating your dinner. Stock turns into soup really easily, and adds subtle flavour to your pasta and rice dishes.

Peel the onion and cut it in half if large, scrape the carrot and place them in a large saucepan or stockpot with 2 litres of water.

Add some other vegetables if you like, perhaps a little celery or celeriac, mushrooms, swede, turnip, courgette or aubergine.

Add the garlic, parsley, bay leaf and a little salt and bring quickly to the boil.

Turn the heat down to medium-low and simmer uncovered for 1 hour.

Strain the stock through a colander.

The boiled vegetables can be added to soups and stews.

Serving Option A
Freeze the stock in pots.

Serving Option D
Return the strained stock to the boil for 15 minutes to give a more concentrated liquid that can be frozen in ice-cube trays.

Serving Option B
Store covered in the coldest part of the fridge for 4–5 days.

Serving Option C
Forget all this and use Marigold Vegetable Bouillon.

Chicken Stock

Makes 350–500ml

- Raw or cooked chicken bones and scraps
- 1 onion
- 1 carrot
- Other vegetable, but not cabbage, potato or tomato (optional)
- 1 bay leaf
- A pinch of saffron
- Salt

Make the stock as soon as possible after the bones become available, otherwise they will lose their flavour. If you have a whole chicken carcass, break it up a little with a rolling pin, as this releases more flavour, but don't shatter it. Be aware that chicken wings make a good but fatty stock.

You could use a duck carcass instead.

Peel the onion and cut it in half, scrape the carrot and place them in a large saucepan or stockpot with 2 litres of water and the chicken bones.

Add any other vegetables you fancy using, but avoid cabbage, potato and tomato.

Add the bay leaf, saffron and a little salt and bring the mixture to the boil. Skim off any scum that rises to the top.

Turn the heat down to medium-low and simmer uncovered for 1 hour.

The boiled vegetables can be added to soups and stews.

Strain the stock through a colander.

When the stock is cool, use a slotted spoon to remove the yellow fat that's risen to the top of the liquid.

In hot weather, you will need to cool the stock as quickly as possible, so sit the pan in an ice bath in the sink.

Serving Option A
Freeze the stock in pots.

Serving Option D
Store covered in the coldest part of the fridge for 4–5 days.

Serving Option B
Return the strained stock to the boil for 15 minutes to give a more concentrated liquid that can be frozen in ice-cube trays.

Serving Option C
Forget all this, and use a stock cube if you really have to, or one of those ready-made organic stocks from the supermarket chilled counter.

MILLS
SH
SKEY
10

THE
BEST
TEQUILA
DON
JULIO
2·50p

GORDON'S
GIN
1·35p

AMARU
CREA
LIQU
SOU
AFRI
1·7

COCONUT
LIQUEUR
1·65p

SOUTHERN
COMFORT
2·00p

CALVADO
APPLE
BRANDY
1·85p

CACHACA
51
FROM
BRAZIL
1·75p

MALIBU
COCONUT
LIQUEUR
1·35p

IR
M
HO
W
2

Turkish Tea

SPECIAL EQUIPMENT

The Turks use a double pot to make their tea, using the water from the bottom pot to dilute the mother liquid from the top one.

Say 'I love you'.
'Beni seni seviyorum.'
Say 'thank you'.
'Çok teşekurler.'
Say 'please'.
'Lutfen.'
Now say it like you mean it.
'LÜTFEN.'
Tell me what you want.
'Beni seni istiyorum.'
You want me?
'Eved.'
You want me now?
'Eved! Eved!'
How do you want me?
'Şule.'
What am I to you?
'Askım, Hayatım, Cigerim'
I am your heart, your life and your liver.

Get up early in the morning. ³/₄ fill the bottom pot with clean water and put on to boil.

Put 4 tablespoons of your best leaf tea in the upper pot, mixing in a bit of Earl Grey if you like.

When the water's on the boil, add 2 tablespoons to the tea leaves, stirring it in to make them moist.

Fit the top pot to the bottom one, put on the lid and simmer the water for about 20 minutes. This allows the tea leaves to steam and swell, releasing all of their flavour.

Half fill the top pot with boiling water, stir the sloppy mixture well, and fit the pots and lid together again and leave to simmer for another 20–30 minutes.

To serve, pour a couple of tablespoons of the mother liquid from the top pot into a small glass, topping it up with boiling water from the bottom pot.

Made like this, a pot of tea can last all day, just keep refilling the bottom pot with water, and make sure the top pot's always about half full.

Turkish Coffee

SPECIAL EQUIPMENT

The Turks use a long-handled kabak and pulverised coffee for this. You can buy the pulverised coffee from supermarkets and all Greek, Turkish and Arabic shops.

Use 1 very heaped tablespoon of coffee per person, and put it in the pot with $^3/_4$ of an espresso cup of water each. If you want sweet coffee, now's the time to add a teaspoon of sugar per person.

Say 'Bismillah'. Give the water/sugar/coffee a stir, and put it on the hob to boil.

Some people repeat this seven times, murmuring all sorts of prayers the while. Only do this if you have an audience who are easily impressed.

When it boils, the froth will rise. Just before it boils over, remove from the heat and knock the pot on a hard surface to get the grounds to settle. Repeat this boiling/knocking process.

Serve very hot in espresso-sized cups.

Leave the bottom $^1/_3$ of the cup as it'll be full of muddy grounds, and you'll look uncool trying to get the bits out of your teeth.

Romantic Water

Per person

- 1 glass of still or sparkling water
- ½ teaspoon of rose water or
orange blossom water (page 38),
or 4–5 cherries

Make sure the water is chilled.

↓

Place in a glass and add
the flower water or fruit to
flavour – if you use fizzy water,
the cherries will float.

↓

If you can't find rose or
orange blossom water in
your local store, any good
chemist will have it.

A Presence Like Rain

There is a kind of spirit that comes
like fresh rain, a water
that carries away to the Ocean
whatever's foul and rotten.

There, water itself gets washed,
and the next year it comes again.

"Where have you been?"
                    "In the sea.
But now I'm ready again to accept all your
Give it to me. Pull off your clothes,
and let me take them."

This is the magnificent work
of those watery souls
who wash us.

How could they shine,
if we were not so impure!

We exhaust their clarity with our silt,
and then the clouds lift them,
and the sun takes them as vapor.

In various molecular ways they go back
to the Ocean. What is meant by this **Water**
is the Spirit of the Enlightened Ones.

Think of these rivers and streams
as medicine shops. Let them take you
to be healed in that wide Water

where even they are cleaned.

Where, look, you can see
their cloudy robes
raining down.

*(Mathnawi,*V, 199-223)

Um sorriso um encontro,
Recordações do campo.

140

Rumi, the Mathnawi, 5, translated by Coleman Barks,
Delicious Laughter, Maypop Books, 1990.

Hoping to Get Lucky

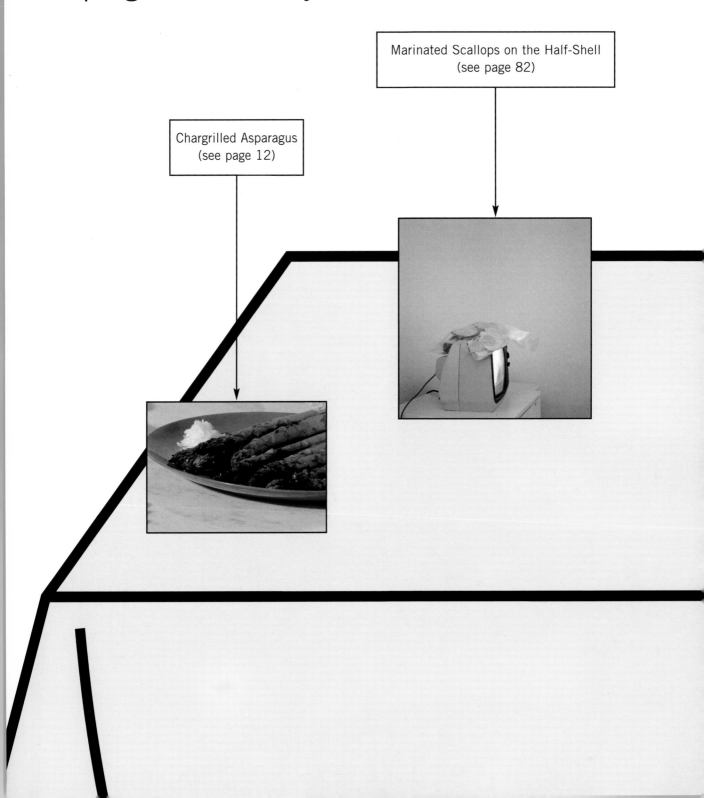

Marinated Scallops on the Half-Shell
(see page 82)

Chargrilled Asparagus
(see page 12)

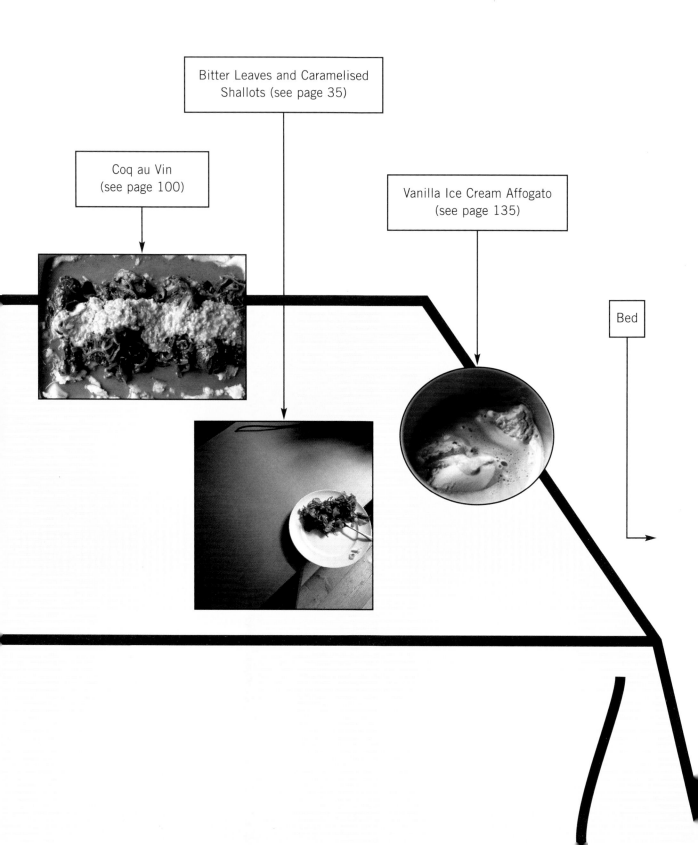

Bitter Leaves and Caramelised
Shallots (see page 35)

Coq au Vin
(see page 100)

Vanilla Ice Cream Affogato
(see page 135)

Bed

Two Couples of Similar Social Standing Who've Known Each Other For Ages, and Are Talking About Holidays

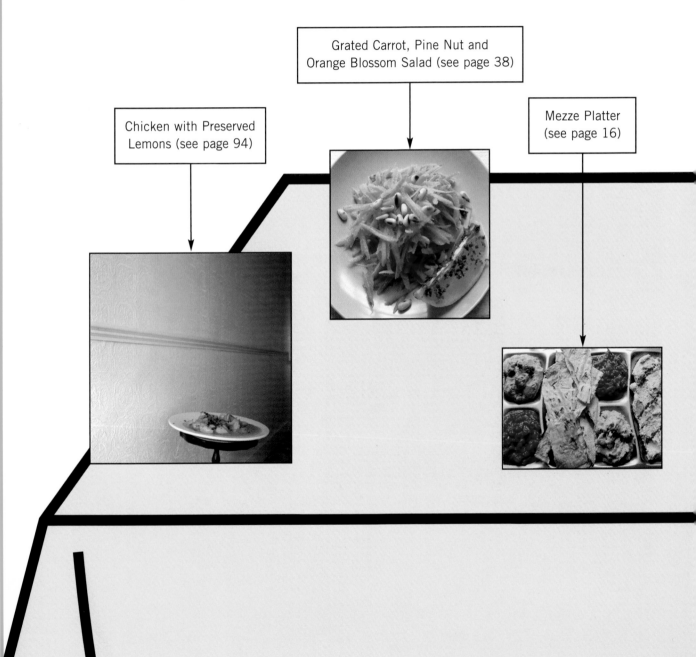

Grated Carrot, Pine Nut and Orange Blossom Salad (see page 38)

Mezze Platter (see page 16)

Chicken with Preserved Lemons (see page 94)

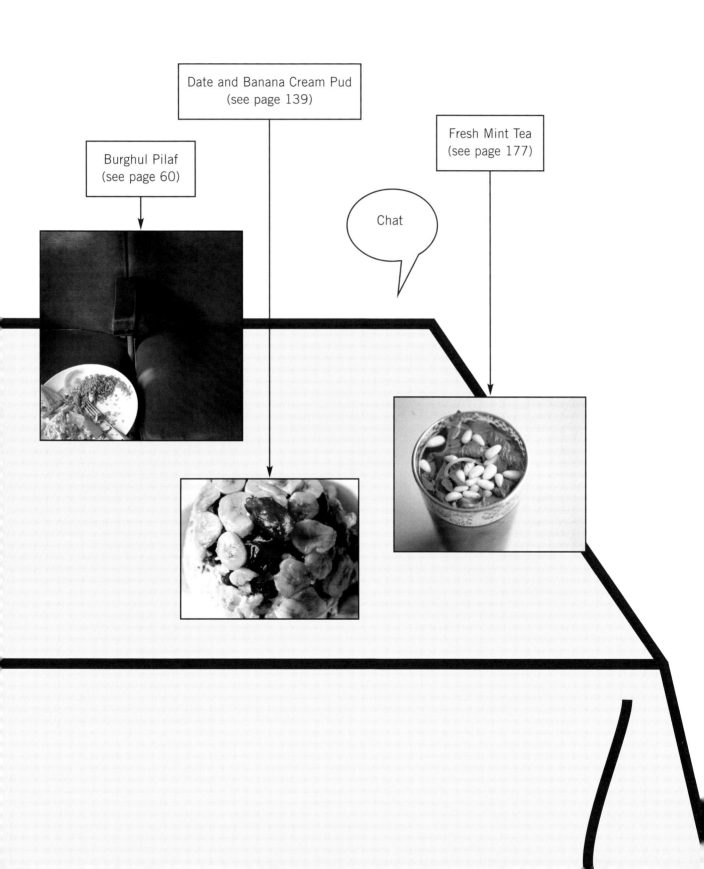

Date and Banana Cream Pud
(see page 139)

Fresh Mint Tea
(see page 177)

Burghul Pilaf
(see page 60)

Chat

Intelligent Documentary TV Dinner

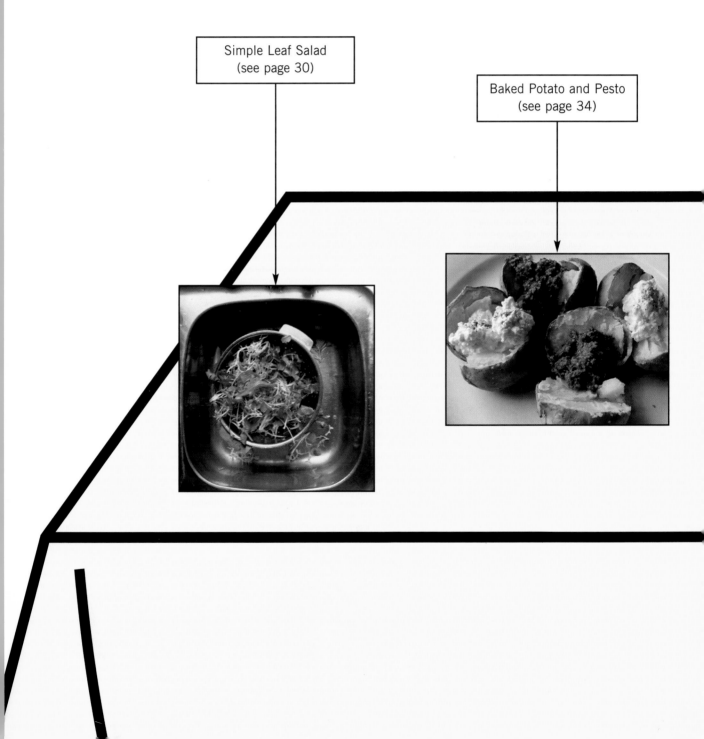

Simple Leaf Salad
(see page 30)

Baked Potato and Pesto
(see page 34)

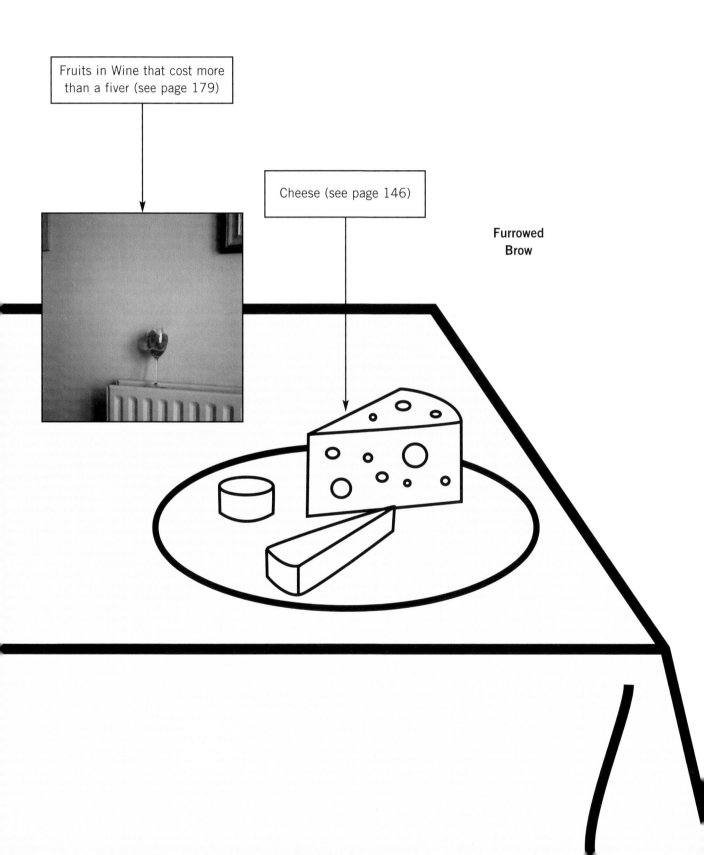

Fruits in Wine that cost more than a fiver (see page 179)

Cheese (see page 146)

Furrowed Brow

Soap TV Dinner

Refried Tomato Spaghetti 'Telephone Exchange'
(see page 162)

Olives (see page 10)

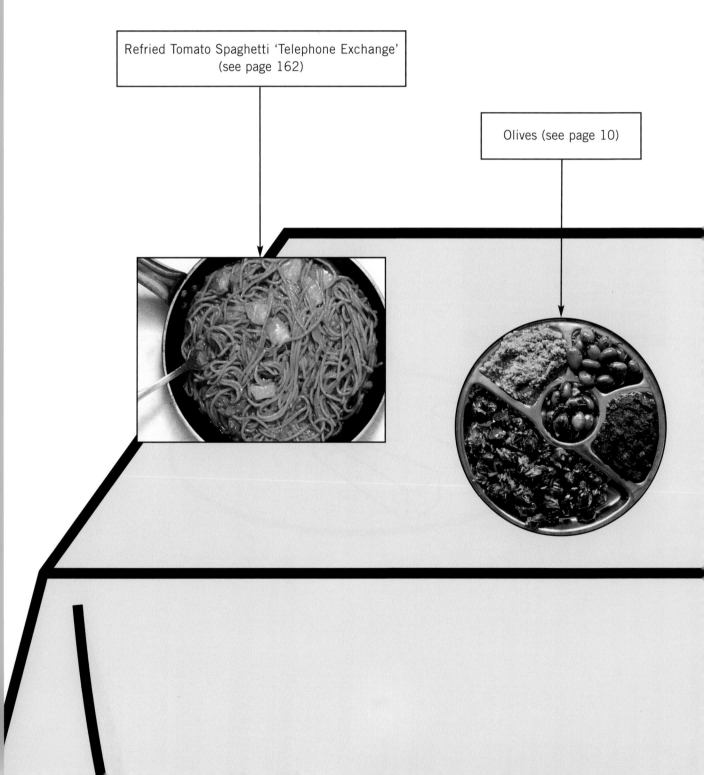

2 Bars of Chocolate that
should have gone into
a Grand Pot au Chocolat
(see page 134)

Release of trouser button

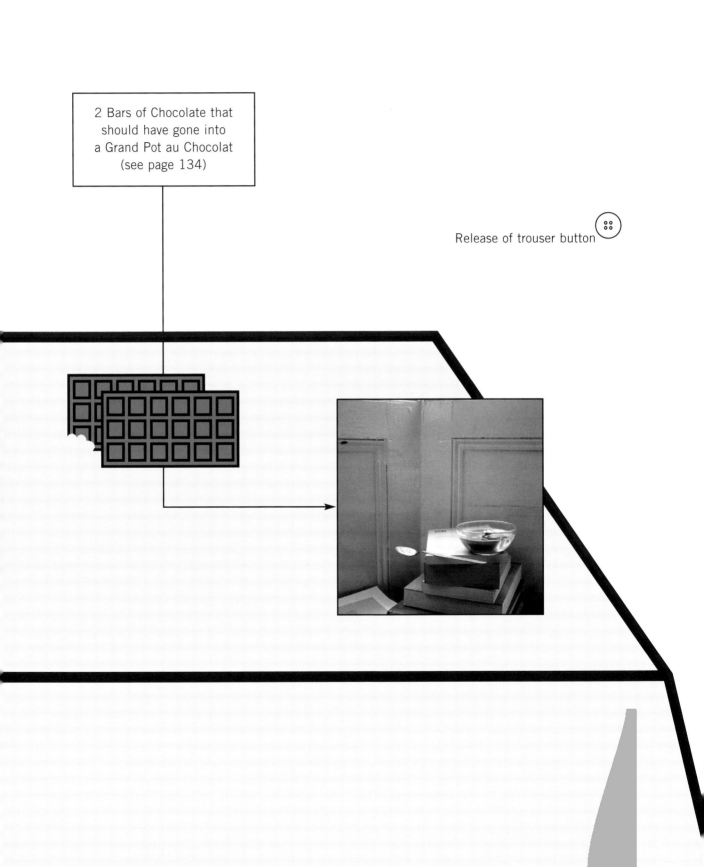

Impressing A Couple You Call Your Friends But Don't Really Know That Well

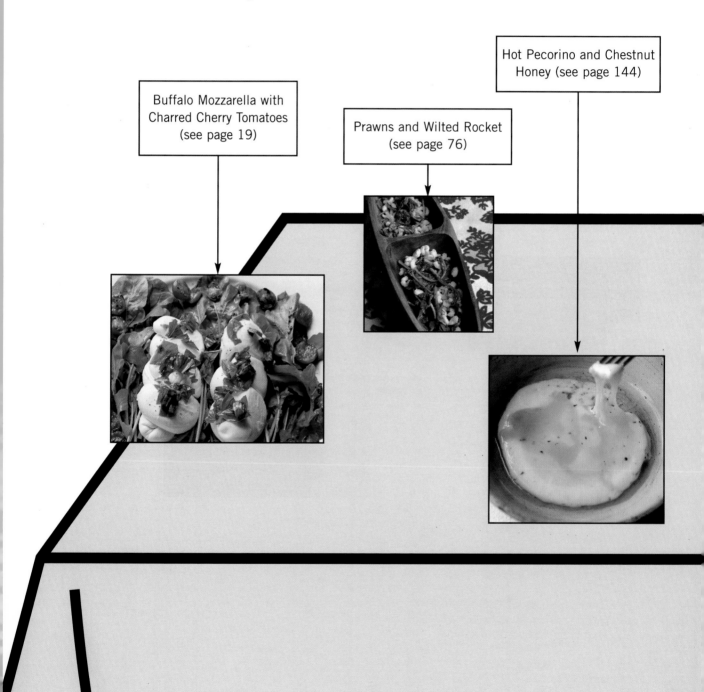

Buffalo Mozzarella with Charred Cherry Tomatoes (see page 19)

Prawns and Wilted Rocket (see page 76)

Hot Pecorino and Chestnut Honey (see page 144)

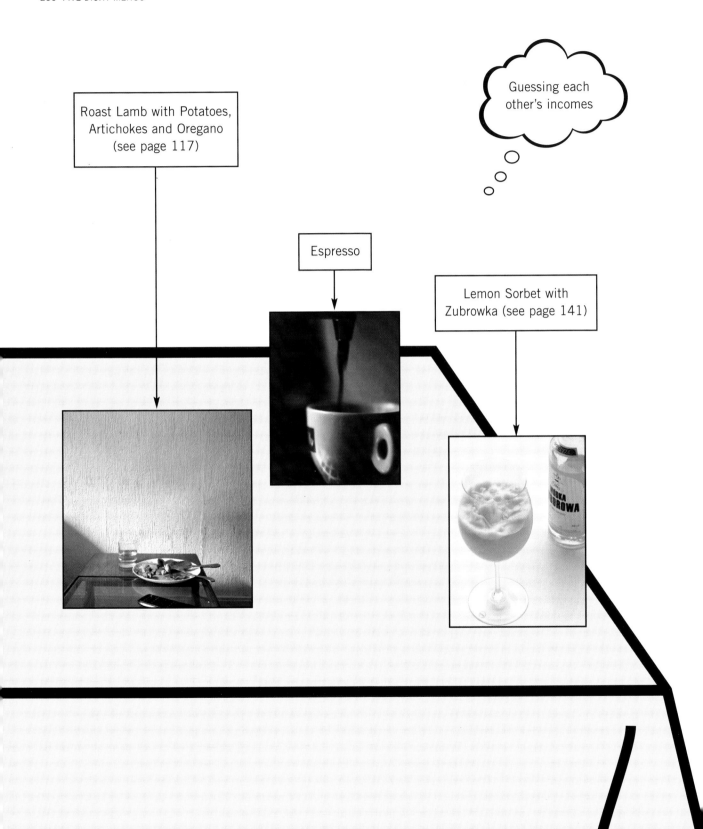

Roast Lamb with Potatoes, Artichokes and Oregano (see page 117)

Espresso

Lemon Sorbet with Zubrowka (see page 141)

Guessing each other's incomes

Figures in italics refer to captions.

Thank you

BEFORE THE BOOK

Michael Alcock, who is to literary agents what Gucci is to leather. Nadia Manuelli, who has impeccable taste, not only for noticing Kevin, but also for marrying Michael. Neale Whittaker, first editor of *Food Illustrated*, who gave Kevin his chance to write and to all current staffers on *Waitrose Food Illustrated* for putting up with the excuses for late copy! All the customers and clients at Realfood, Joy, Love and Like This, who put Kevin in a position where anyone might actually be interested in what he has to say.

DURING THE BOOK

Jenni Muir for her inspiration, intelligence, technical know-how and recipe writing. Everyone at Realfood, Joy, Love and Like This, who enjoyed the fact the Kevin wasn't around while he was writing, but were too polite to say so. My wife Frances Ndegwa, whose charm, good sense, patience and sheer beauty sets her apart from the rest of the world; and our three amazing kids, Theo, Phoebe and Tommy, who never cease to surprise everyone with their gifts. Simon and Dad for being there when I needed help. Stephanie Nash, Anthony Michael, David Hitner and Alexia Cox at Michael Nash, who have designed this book, and whose creative thinking, lateral approach and professional expertise have made working on DISHY so joyful and special. All the photographers, whose sharp eyes and trigger fingers have produced such arresting and amazing images.

AFTER THE BOOK

The entire team at Hodder & Stoughton.
You, for buying it.

ALSO

All the people past, present and future, who have worked at Realfood, Joy, Love and Like This.

Realfood, 14 Clifton Road, Little Venice,
London W9 1SS. For branches, call 020 7266 1162
or e-mail realfood@dircon.co.uk
www.dishy.net

design@michaelnash.co.uk

Some Basic Kitchen Kit

- A non-stick chargrill pan or griddle pan.
- A large pan, big enough to cook pasta for a party.
- A small pan, for heating up a can of beans.
- A large non-stick frying pan, for a big fry-up.
- A small non-stick frying pan, for a small fry-up.
- An electric kettle. A good cook nearly always starts cooking by putting the kettle on – lots of dishes need boiling water. Tough or what?
- Two chopping boards, one for raw meats and fish and the other for smelly stuff, like garlic, onions and chile if you like them, or vegetables.
- A pair of scissors – most of the things that need cutting in Dishy can be cut with sharp scissors.
- A sharp kitchen knife – for the things that aren't easy to cut with scissors.
- A vegetable peeler. This will save you lots of time.
- A big colander, for draining pasta and washing salads.
- A plastic bowl and lid. Do they still have Tupperware parties? How are you supposed to wear that stuff?
- A mister. Misters are in most supermarket homeware sections and all garden centres and DIY stores, and cost less than a fiver.

£10 off when you spend £50 or more on Irradial stainless steel cookware at Habitat

Just as possessing antique linen sheets and hand-made silk pyjamas doesn't guarantee you'll be good in bed, owning the flashiest kitchen kit won't make you a great cook. Flashy geegaws and funky gadgets are all very well, and some of them may actually save you some time and effort, but there's no getting around the fact that if you fancy getting real about food, you need proper pots and pans.

All of the dishes shown in DISHY were cooked by real people in home kitchens all over London using simple, sturdy Irradial pans. They each had a small saucepan, a frying pan and a stockpot. Irradial cookware looks cool, yet distributes heat evenly, just like the best professional pans do. You can stick them in the oven and dishwasher, and it's easy enough to keep them looking clean. Those nice people at Habitat are offering all you DISHY people a good discount on the Irradial range. (As if you need another excuse to Spend! Spend! Spend!).

habitat

Please fill in your name and address details below

Your name _____

Nickname _____

Address _____

_____

Postcode _____

Email _____

Favourite pet _____

How would you like to be contacted by Habitat in the future: ☐ e-mail ☐ by post. Please tick this box if you do not wish to receive any further information from Habitat ☐.

£10 OFF WHEN YOU SPEND £50 OR MORE ON IRRADIAL STAINLESS STEEL COOKWARE AT HABITAT. OFFER ENDS 31 DECEMBER 2000.

To claim your £10 discount, simply hand this voucher in at your nearest Habitat store when you purchase Irradial stainless steel cookware to the value of £50 or more.

For the location of your nearest Habitat store and opening hours please call 0845 6010740 or visit the Habitat website at www.habitat.net. For details of specific product availability please contact your nearest store.